T0286201

Rise
and
Shine

Rise and Shine

Kate Oliver &
Toby Oliver

PIATKUS

PIATKUS

First published in Great Britain in 2021 by Piatkus

3 5 7 9 10 8 6 4

ISBN: 978-0-349-42935-9

Typeset in Swift by M Rules
Printed and bound in Great Britain by
Clays Ltd, Elcograf S.p.A.

Papers used by Piatkus are from well-managed forests
and other responsible sources.

Piatkus
An imprint of
Little, Brown Book Group
Carmelite House
50 Victoria Embankment
London EC4Y 0DZ

An Hachette UK Company
www.hachette.co.uk

www.littlebrown.co.uk

To our parents, Peter and Yvonne Oliver, without whom there would have been no mornings, let alone the chance to shine.

Contents

Part 3
Rising and shining every morning

Introduction

Why it's time to wake up and find your S.H.I.N.E.

'This is a wonderful day. I've
never seen this one before.'

– Maya Angelou

Good morning!

In our busy lives, it's all too easy to wake up feeling overwhelmed and rush into the day, pulled and pushed around by all the people, tasks and demands facing us.

We wrote this book to help you shine through and rise above life's changes and challenges. To be your best self, whatever the weather. We made it for you to keep on your bedside table, to motivate and inspire you each morning.

We're Kate Oliver, a chartered psychologist and executive coach, and Toby Oliver, a therapist and yoga and meditation teacher. We're also sister and brother.

Rise and Shine is based on the latest scientific research as well as age-old traditions, blended with the insights we've gathered from the more than five decades of professional experience we have between us.

We designed the S.H.I.N.E. method as a flexible way to help you create a new and positive morning routine: one that gets your mornings off to the best possible start and sets you up for a happy, healthy and successful day where you feel great and flourish.

The S.H.I.N.E. approach is made up of five categories of practices we recommend for an uplifting and energising start to your day: Silence, Happiness, Intention, Nourishment and Exercise.

In each section, we have curated six simple but powerful tools to help you to shine, sharing with you where they come from, why they work and how to use them.

The 30 S.H.I.N.E. practices you're about to discover have not only transformed our own mornings, but also the mornings of many other people we've worked with over the years, enabling them to improve their wellbeing, mental health, emotional resilience and productivity. As a result, these practices have transformed their lives.

We know they can do the same for you.

By starting your morning well, you're giving yourself the best possible chance of a wonderful day ahead. Because how you begin your morning sets the tone for the rest of your day.

Rise and Shine is for you if you want to change your life, morning by morning. To set yourself up to thrive.

Whether or not you think of yourself as a 'morning person', this book is for you.

Whether you 'hate' mornings or 'love' them, this book is for you.

However 'old' or 'young' you are, this book is for you.

Whether you work at home or travel to work, this book is for you.

If your days are a frenzied rush of activity, this book is for you.

If your days feel aimless and lacking in structure, this book is for you.

If your mornings are busy with work, family and other commitments, this book is for you.

Now is the perfect time to begin. Picking up this book has been your first step towards rediscovering your shine. Seize the day, and you'll soon see the results.

It's your time to rise and shine!

Kate and Toby

Part 1

Starting to shine

'They always say time changes things, but you actually have to change them yourself.'

– Andy Warhol, *The Philosophy of Andy Warhol: From A to B and Back Again*

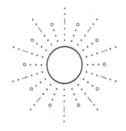

Chapter 1

Our stories

How we discovered the way to S.H.I.N.E.

'When you arise in the morning, think of
what a precious privilege it is to be alive –
to breathe, to think, to enjoy, to love.'

– Marcus Aurelius

Many of us don't share Marcus Aurelius's first thoughts
on waking and it certainly wasn't always like that for
us. Our mornings used to be *very* different. Like many
people, we used to have unhelpful and unhealthy starts
to our days. Here are our personal stories of how we
turned that around to create morning routines that
give us better balance and more resilience, and get our

days off to a great start. In other words, how we learned to S.H.I.N.E.

How it all started

As an older sister and younger brother, who grew up sharing a room with bunk beds, we developed our own unhelpful morning routine early in life. It largely consisted of Toby, who slept on the bottom bunk, kicking Kate's mattress and calling out, 'Kate, are you awake?' with increasing ferocity until she grumpily shouted, 'No, shut up! I'm sleeping!' This set us up perfectly for a day full of squabbling, arguing and fighting.

Even when we later got separate bedrooms, we continued our pattern of arguing and fighting from the minute we woke up until last thing at night – much to our parents' despair.

It took several years before we stopped irritating each other, and even longer before we each discovered the life-changing benefits of a S.H.I.N.E. routine.

Kate's story

For a number of years, I had struggled with anxiety and depression. I used to sleep badly and wake in the early hours of the morning with my heart racing and my mind whirring, ruminating on things that had happened and worrying about the day ahead. I was often exhausted before the time came to force myself out of bed.

As a trained psychologist, I was really good at helping others and I knew the theory, but I couldn't quite seem to put it into practice to help myself. This made me feel even worse about things – I was scared of being 'found out' – and some days it seemed like I was only just staying afloat. It felt like my mornings were broken – and so was I.

A few years ago, after a relationship break-up, I hit rock bottom and decided that things had to change. I started a disciplined self-coaching programme. Every morning I would wake up and use a combination of positive affirmations, structured journaling and learning from inspirational podcasts. At first it was hard to do, but I stuck with it, initially because I was desperate to find anything that might help me to feel better. After a few weeks, though, I began to notice the positive differences this new morning routine was making. My anxiety levels were dropping, and I was able to be more resilient, focused and productive during the day.

Over time, I experimented with new and different practices, building in breathing exercises, meditation and other forms of movement, too, such as shaking (more on this in chapter 7). My life was transforming, and not just on a personal level: I was enjoying my work more and getting far better results with the people I was working with. My relationships were also improving, because I was calmer and more positive to be around. People spontaneously told me that I seemed much happier, more grounded, radiant; they said they were inspired by the changes in me and asked me what I had done to create these.

I started to share some of my morning techniques with my training and coaching clients, and I witnessed the difference these practices made to their lives, too. That's why I decided to write this book – so that as many people as possible can benefit.

As a freelance consultant running my own business, my work pattern is very varied from day to day. Sometimes, I am working from home all day and have to motivate myself to get going. On other days, I might have a really early start, travelling into clients' offices, or perhaps working overseas, focusing on the needs of others all day in a training room. Whatever I'm doing on any given day, my morning practice is now an integral part of how I start it. I want my day to start well, so I only allow myself positive inputs upon waking (no reading the news or my emails first thing).

Nowadays, my morning practices come from a sense of inspiration rather than desperation, because I know they set me up to shine throughout my day. Of course, I'm only human, so on those days when I do wake up feeling more challenged, my S.H.I.N.E. routine helps me to nurture, rebalance and focus myself for the day ahead. I vary the techniques I use to keep it interesting, but there are key elements that always form my morning routine's foundations, even on those days when I have only a small amount of time to dedicate to it. I recently turned fifty, and it's amazing to know that I have the power to create happy, healthy and successful days each and every morning for the rest of my life.

Toby's story

I used to love mornings as a child. I couldn't wait to get up and get going, because I was so excited and impatient to get the day under way. I just wanted someone to play with, and I couldn't understand why no one else seemed to share my excitement.

This pattern continued into adulthood. I would regularly find myself the first to wake, regardless of how late I'd got to bed the night before. I would fidget and fuss, unable to get back to sleep and 'accidentally' wake up my poor husband, frequently finding myself repeating that well-worn, childhood phrase: 'Are you awake yet?'

Then, several years ago, life got busier, and work got more and more demanding and less and less enjoyable. I was juggling a very stressful senior management role with setting up a new business. On top of this, several people I loved were going through horribly tough times. It started to become too much. My mental and physical health were suffering. I found myself struggling to wake up and swearing at the alarm when it went off. I had to make myself crawl into the shower, resentfully force on my work suit and – on a good day – wolf down some toast as I ran out of the door.

I dreaded what 'horrors' yet another day held in store for me and my loved ones.

It's fair to say my mornings didn't start well, and the rest of the day was usually just as bad, if not worse. I was barely awake, let alone conscious. It felt like a non-stop rush from the minute my eyes opened to the second I collapsed exhaustedly into bed at night. My enthusiasm had gone, my energy was almost non-existent. My life had become all whine and no shine.

Then, one day, waiting for the kettle to boil, I felt myself at breaking point. My instinct was to run away and hide – from work, from life, from all the stress I was under. I had been attending Dru Yoga class one evening a week, and something inside me said, 'Why not do a bit of yoga now?' I decided to give it a go, right there in the kitchen, and it made me feel a bit better.

I soon found myself doing a simple yoga practice every morning. It changed how I felt going into even the busiest or 'worst' of days, and was often the highlight. Once I noticed this, I decided to set my dreaded alarm a few minutes earlier to fit more yoga in. I was slowly waking up to the difference it was making – not only to how I felt about the day ahead, but also to how I was able to deal with that day. I was starting to rebuild resilience and find some much-needed balance. I was starting to feel more in control and less in despair.

Ultimately, it was discovering the transformative benefits of this simple morning routine that convinced me to train to become a yoga teacher in order to share these benefits with others.

In time, I began to include more of the techniques you'll learn about in this book – such as joy (rediscovering my long-neglected love of reading), meditation, affirmations, learning and mapping your day. These were transformational, and my mornings became exciting again. I found myself growing more confident, coping better and becoming able to take my life in the direction in which I wanted it to go.

I know that without these morning practices, I wouldn't have had the confidence, creative energy or motivation to fundamentally change my life. I wouldn't have had the courage to leave my well-paid job, set up a theatre company (let alone produce a West End show), teach yoga and train as a therapist – or even write this book.

My morning routine brings a sense of structure and certainty back into my days. I now treasure the precious moments of silence and calm with myself after I wake. There's plenty of time and energy for work, and people to play with later in the day. And each day brings the chance of wonderful new adventures I never previously imagined possible.

Our new story

'I have always been delighted at the prospect of a new day, a fresh try, one more start, with perhaps a bit of magic waiting somewhere behind the morning.'

– J. B. Priestley

Our *Rise and Shine* collaboration started to take shape after we accidentally ended up on a personal development workshop together. This was a slightly daunting prospect for a brother and sister, but we pushed through our initial awkwardness. And thankfully we grew even closer as a result, learning more about who we had both become as adults.

Shortly afterwards, we got talking about ideas we had for books we wanted to write to share our personal and professional experiences with others. It was at this point that we discovered how important our morning routines were to each of us. We discussed how they have helped us improve our mental health and navigate the many changes in our personal and professional lives. We also talked about how sharing our routines with them had helped many of our clients. And so the idea for *Rise and Shine* was born.

One of the lovely things about getting together to work on this book is that we've learned new practices from each other to bring into our own morning routines.

This is our first collaboration, and we're confident it can help you as much as it has helped us. As brother and sister, we certainly wouldn't have been able to work together so harmoniously without the amazing benefits we both get from our morning practices.

Introducing S.H.I.N.E.

S.H.I.N.E. is our approach to building a positive morning routine that will boost your mental, emotional and physical wellbeing, setting you up for a happy, healthy and successful day.

S.H.I.N.E. stands for Silence, Happiness, Intention, Nourishment and Exercise.

We want you to rise and S.H.I.N.E. Our years of combined experience have taught us that there are some key foundations that, when consciously put in place at the start of each day, enable people to feel good and be at their best.

S.H.I.N.E. is not a one-size-fits-all approach. With this book, you will learn how to create the right blend of Silence, Happiness, Intention, Nourishment and Exercise for you, by choosing the practices that work for you and fit in with your life. This flexibility lies at the heart of the S.H.I.N.E. approach.

S is for silence

Once we get into our day, there are many people and things clamouring for our attention. This can feel pretty overwhelming at times. Bringing moments of stillness, peace and reflection into your morning helps centre and calm you for the day ahead, whatever it may bring.

H is for happiness

Our morning mood sets the tone for the day. So if you begin by feeling positive and uplifted, you can move into the day with a smile on your face and cope resiliently with any challenges you may face.

I is for intention

When we don't know what we want to achieve from the day, it's easy to get distracted, lose focus and end up feeling demoralised. This is why it is important that you get clear on your intentions, so you can *create your day* rather than letting *it* create *you.*

N is for nourishment

We are living systems and we need energy to thrive. What you choose to feed both your body and mind when you wake up has a huge impact on the rest of your day. A healthy and nourishing physical and mental morning 'diet' will reinvigorate you for the day ahead.

E is for exercise

Our lives are increasingly sedentary, and we need to get moving to wake ourselves up and create vitality for the day ahead. This gives you the flexibility and strength you need to get through your day with ease.

'We took our time to carefully curate the thirty practices that make-up the S.H.I.N.E. approach. We began by sharing those that we'd personally benefited from, as well as ones we knew worked well for our clients and that were backed up by scientific evidence. It was fascinating to find out how many of the practices we had in common, and even more exciting to discover new practices from each other. We tried and tested each and every one, discarding any that were too complicated or time-consuming. This left us with a final challenge: how to present the practices in a way that was both helpful and practical. It was clear that the practices fell naturally into groups – for example, the ones that help bring clarity and focus, those that are calming and centring, and those that bring joy and positivity to our mornings. We both went away to reflect on how best to present our approach. Kate had the final inspiration, early one morning while sitting in her car. As the sun began to rise, she noticed the light shining off every surface, and an idea began to take shape. The notion of the 'shine' acronym allowed everything to fall into place. The practices fitted perfectly into the five sections: silence (S), happiness (H), intention (I), nourishment (N) and exercise (E). And so the S.H.I.N.E. approach was born.'

– Kate & Toby

Chapter 2

This is your wake-up call

It's time for you to rise and S.H.I.N.E.

'Arise, awake . . .'

– Swami Vivekananda

It's time to wake up!

Some people open their eyes and are full of enthusiasm for the day to come; others groan and yank the covers back over their heads. How does the day start for you? Do you rise and shine?

Your morning doesn't have to be ruled by:

- a rush of things to do before leaving the house

- a long, drawn-out series of distractions that stop you from getting up and on with your day
- worrying and feeling miserable about either yesterday or the day ahead

You can choose to start your day in a different way.

Your morning routine starts the moment you wake up, with your first thought of the day. It matters. A study by the Wharton School at the University of Pennsylvania and the Fisher College of Business at Ohio State University found that people who started the day in a bad mood finished the day in a bad – or even worse – mood, whereas those who started the day in a good mood often ended up even happier as the day went on. So your morning mood lasts and often amplifies as you go through your day. (You will find details of all the research evidence we refer to throughout the book, along with further reading recommendations, in the Notes and References section on pages 223–239.)

We know that numerous high achievers in all walks of life – from business and politics to the arts and sport – credit their morning routine as being instrumental to their success. In the words of Michelle Obama, 'We need to do a better job of putting ourselves higher on our own "to-do" list.'

We also know, both from our personal experience and from many years of working with hundreds of people, that having a consistent and constructive morning routine can reduce stress and anxiety, build resilience and make you happier and more productive.

Some of the key benefits from having a positive morning routine include:

- feeling calmer and more in control
- enjoying enhanced wellbeing
- experiencing higher energy levels
- finding a greater sense of meaning and purpose
- becoming more productive and achieving more

That's because the way you start your morning affects how you think, feel and act during the rest of the day. This, in turn, has a major impact on your overall wellbeing, mental health, energy and productivity.

Just as each moment shapes the next, each morning shapes the day.

It's simple: how you start your day is the way your day is going to be.

Is your current morning routine helping you?

Whether or not you realise it, you already *have* a morning routine: it's all those things you do every morning without fail, like groaning at your alarm, checking your phone, brushing your teeth, taking a shower, eating breakfast, catching up on the news or scanning social media.

Your routine will include many familiar things you got into the habit of doing years ago, perhaps in childhood, and you may never have stopped to question these habits as you've grown and your life has changed.

Some of them may be helpful; some of them, perhaps less so. Some are simply time-traps. It's amazing how often we get in our own way without even realising it, by getting caught in patterns of thinking, feeling and doing that have become invisible to us, even as they trip us up.

How did you start today?

We invite you to pause for a moment and reflect on how you started your morning today. Pay attention to what you did, what you were thinking and how you were feeling.

How about yesterday morning? And the day before that?

Some people find it helpful to close their eyes to do this. Others prefer to jot down on paper some notes about what they remember.

What patterns or habits do you notice? How conscious were you of these at the time? Were they helpful? How well did they set you up for the day ahead?

Chances are, many of the things you do each morning

are so automatic that you barely notice they're happening, let alone think about doing them. They have become your morning habits and together they make up your 'accidental' morning routine.

Is this routine working for you? Or might it be holding you back or getting in your way, without you realising it? Could it be bringing you down instead of lifting you up? *Is it allowing you to rise and shine?*

If not, it's time to make a change.

The dawning of a new you

Have you ever wondered why sunsets and sunrises are the most photographed of natural scenes?

It's not simply because they are beautiful. They speak to us in a primal way. Before we had artificial lighting, our lives were ruled by the rising and setting of the sun.

Sunrise marks a transition: the moving from one state to another; the ending of one thing and the beginning of another. A new day and a new beginning. The dawning of a new day brings with it new possibilities, and a shift in gear from rest to action.

This is your opportunity to seize the day: to start as you mean to go on, and to make time for yourself, so you can feel and be at your best for the day ahead and all it brings. Consciously creating your morning can shape your entire day, and you can do it by simply doing a few small things differently when you first awake.

'A few years ago, I taught on a yoga retreat in Norway. It was a wonderful experience apart from one thing – it never got dark, because during the summer months the sun doesn't set. I found this so strange and really challenging. How was I to know the difference between day and night? I asked my friend and co-teacher how she coped. She explained that we still have the same twenty-four hours in a day during the long, dark winters and the endless summers. We get to choose how to spend them. We not only have the ability to do this – we have the *responsibility* to establish a rhythm for our own days. It slowly dawned on me that this was what my morning S.H.I.N.E. routine did for me. Realising this restored my sense of structure and balance. My day began when I wanted, and I could rise and shine, regardless of the season.'

– Toby

Time for change

It's simple.

If you want your life to change, you either have to start doing things differently or start doing different things.

If you want your days to change, you need to get your mornings off to a new and positive start.

How this book works

In the rest of this chapter, we'll show you how to create space for your new morning S.H.I.N.E. routine. As you'll discover, it's not just easy – it's also enjoyable and highly effective.

In Chapters 3 to 7, you will find your S.H.I.N.E. toolkit, containing the 30 S.H.I.N.E. practices. All of them are easy to understand, quick to learn, practical and enjoyable to use.

For each practice, you'll learn what it is, why it works (including the latest scientific evidence) and get easy-to-follow guidance on how to do it. Plus, we share insights from our personal and professional experience of using the practices.

All the practices can be completed in ten minutes and under (and some in as little as sixty seconds), meaning they can make a difference to your day without getting in your way. We've tried them all ourselves, and also successfully shared them with many of our clients and students. We know they work.

In Chapter 8, we show you how to simply and easily build your new morning S.H.I.N.E. routine, and share a couple of sample routines to get you started.

In Chapter 9, you'll learn why a morning routine is even more important in times of change, challenge and uncertainty. We will teach you how to use the S.H.I.N.E. approach to create a balanced sense of wellbeing when life gets tough. This includes our suggestions of routines to help you with specific needs and challenges. For example, you'll learn what works best: when you've had a bad night's sleep; when you have a long, busy day ahead; when you are feeling overwhelmed; and much more.

Chapter 10 will help you to get started and keep going. You will learn how to form new habits and stay motivated. We give you our 'Ten Simple Steps to S.H.I.N.E.'.

Finally, in the Resources, we share a range of practical tools and tips to help you on your journey to S.H.I.N.E. This includes examples of our own personal S.H.I.N.E. routines, along with a blank planner you can use to create yours.

Find your way to S.H.I.N.E.

The S.H.I.N.E. approach is not a one-size-fits-all formula. We want to give you flexibility and choice.

In this book, you won't find lists telling you what you must eat or how you have to dress. There won't be pages of impossibly complicated tips that are supposed to somehow help you save time. And we're not going to tell you to do anything that makes you feel uncomfortable. You don't need lots of money, specialist equipment or other people.

You already have everything you need to succeed.

Some of the practices we share here may be things you're already familiar with, or things you already feel you do. The beauty of the S.H.I.N.E. method is that you'll learn to appreciate how to do these things *consistently*, and with conscious intention. And you'll discover how combining them with other practices to create a daily S.H.I.N.E. routine enables you to reap their full benefits.

We want you to be able to craft your own bespoke morning S.H.I.N.E. routine by choosing the elements that feel right for you at this time in your life. Different practices will appeal to different people, so we have chosen a range of practices to suit different lifestyles, personalities and needs. We are confident you'll find plenty here to help you rise and shine.

Keep an open mind. Who knows? In time, you may find practices that didn't initially hold much appeal start to make more sense to you as life moves on and you change.

It's *your* morning. Be willing to experiment and try out a few things to find what works best.

Make time

To begin with, you need to create a little bit of time in your morning, just for you. Some people call this 'me' time, others refer to it as 'self-care' time. You might want to think of it as making an appointment with yourself. See this as charging your batteries, in order to light the day ahead. It's important.

You might be thinking, 'But I'm already busy and my mornings are full, with no time left to spare!' We understand. That used to be our view, too. Trust us, it's so much easier than you think – and the results are well worth it.

'As a working mum, running my own business, I didn't think it would be possible to find any time for myself in the mornings. But as I started to try out some of the S.H.I.N.E. practices, I realised how much time I had previously wasted worrying and procrastinating each morning. I had more time than I thought – and the small things I started doing differently had a transformative effect on the rest of my day.'

– Kate

A reality check

All you need to get started is to find a few uninterrupted minutes in your morning.

Decide what is realistic and helpful for you. It might simply be a case of making different choices about how you use your time upon waking (for example, using the time you currently spend browsing on your phone, worrying or watching TV). Or it might mean setting your alarm a little bit earlier.

You could try cutting back on TV, Netflix or late-night phone surfing the evening before to allow you to get to sleep a bit sooner, making it easier to wake up a little earlier than usual. Build up to it: start by setting your alarm five to ten minutes earlier and see the difference it makes to have those precious extra minutes for yourself at the start of your day.

Make a start

We recommend creating, as far as possible, a distraction-free space for yourself.

So put your phone on 'do not disturb' mode – ideally, before you start looking at emails, messages and updates – and shut off all sources of digital distraction. Reduce competition for your attention in your environment: try to find a space where you can focus, just for these few minutes. This could be in your bedroom, somewhere else in your home or, depending on the weather, even outside.

> 'My new morning routine first began in the kitchen by doing yoga and gazing out at the dawn while I was waiting for the kettle to boil. The rest of the house was still asleep, and I appreciated the space and time to myself. I loved the way I was able to seamlessly integrate new practices into my existing morning routine.'
>
> – Toby

Start small, like we did. Find just five to ten minutes where you can be undisturbed and try out one or two of the S.H.I.N.E. practices.

Give yourself permission to try something new.

As you look through the practices, you will probably find that some of them particularly resonate with you. That's OK, but it's also helpful to be mindful that, when choosing, we often resist what we need most. So, you might also benefit from those practices that have the *least* initial appeal for you. You may well find that these grow on you as you start to use them.

If you're not sure where to begin, don't worry. At the start of each S.H.I.N.E. section, we suggest a couple of practices that are good first steps. These are the practices we regularly find are helpful starting points when working with our clients. They are simple and effective, creating a solid foundation for you to start rising and shining through your new morning S.H.I.N.E. routine. But you may prefer to choose others. Don't get hung up on getting it 'right' – just make a start.

Ahead of time

We have specifically chosen practices that do not require much in terms of preparation, money or equipment. However, for a few of the practices, you will need to have some basic things ready, like a pen, a notebook, a candle, water, a timer, something to play music on and food for breakfast.

It can be helpful to decide what practices you'll use

the following morning. That way you can get anything you need ready the night before so you can get going straight away when you wake up. For example, if you want to practise learning, find an inspiring podcast to listen to the night before; if you want to practise yoga, get your mat out before you go to bed; if you want to practise meditation, make sure you have identified a space in which to do this. The fewer barriers you have to getting started, the easier it is to do so.

Give it time

At first, your new morning routine will take conscious effort and probably won't feel totally natural. This is part of the process of change – you are choosing to move outside your comfort zone. It's not about doing it perfectly; it's about doing something different.

It's what you do every day that matters, much more than what you do sometimes. The key is in the repetition. That's why they're called 'practices' – you have to practise them regularly.

The great thing about these practices is that, unlike caffeine, alcohol or junk food, the more you do them, the greater the effects, and the better you feel.

So stick with it and experience the power of the changes you are making. Allow yourself the opportunity to grow brighter and more radiant every day.

Part 2

The 30 S.H.I.N.E. practices

'The first hour of the morning is the rudder of the day.'

– Henry Ward Beecher

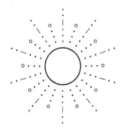

The 30 S.H.I.N.E. practices

Here is an overview of the 30 S.H.I.N.E. practices that make up our toolkit.

S	H	I	N	E
Silence	**Happiness**	**Intention**	**Nourishment**	**Exercise**
Breathing	Hugging	Alarm clock	Breakfast	Body scan
Candle gazing	Gratitude	Creative visualisation	Learning	Dancing
Free writing	Joy	Goal-setting	Mantra	Making your bed
Meditation	Mirror work	Mapping your day	Nature	Movement
Mindfulness	Positive affirmations	Mindset	Sunlight	Shaking
Structured journaling	Smiling	'To-be' list	Water	Yoga

Chapter 3

Silence

'In silence there is eloquence. Stop weaving
and see how the pattern improves.'

– Rumi

Silence is indeed golden. In a loud and demanding world, increasingly full of distractions, creating moments of peace benefits both your brain and your body. It's well evidenced that building silence into your morning routine brings calm and clarity before entering the busy-ness and noisiness of your day.

The six S.H.I.N.E. practices in this section offer you a range of ways to bring stillness, peace and reflection into your morning.

- Breathing (page 37)
- Candle gazing (page 43)
- Free writing (page 47)
- Meditation (page 52)
- Mindfulness (page 58)
- Structured journaling (page 62)

Flick through and choose one of the practices to get going with. If you are not sure where to begin, we often find breathing and structured journaling are good places to start.

Breathing

> 'When the breath wanders the mind
> also is unsteady. But when the breath
> is calmed the mind too will be still.'

– Hatha Yoga Pradipika, *Swami Swatmarama*

Breathing keeps us alive; it's the first and last thing we ever do. Whether we're aware of it or not, our bodies keeps inhaling and exhaling, and every day we take approximately 20,000 breaths.

Breathing is important for two reasons:

- Our in-breath supplies the whole of the body and its organs, including the brain, with oxygen. This is vital for our survival. Oxygen cannot be stored and has to be continuously replenished.
- We use our out-breath to get rid of toxic carbon dioxide – a natural waste product of respiration.

Our breath is also the link between our bodies and our minds. The way we breathe affects and reflects both our physical energy and health and how we think and feel.

When we are stressed or anxious, our breath tends to become quick, shallow, tight and irregular. This activates the body's stress response – the 'fight or flight' survival instinct that is designed to protect us. As a result, our minds become increasingly unsettled and agitated, and we feel more tense and anxious.

The opposite is also true; when we're calm and relaxed, our breath naturally steadies and becomes deeper and slower. And this, in turn, activates the body's 'rest and digest' response, which helps us be more at ease, open and creative.

The good news is that we can intentionally use our breath as a tool to change our physical and emotional state. By deliberately breathing deeply and slowly, we bring clarity and focus, refreshing and relaxing our minds and our bodies.

Conscious, calm breathing like this has been scientifically proven to have many benefits including:

- lowering anxiety and reducing stress
- supporting good mental health and wellbeing
- reducing blood pressure
- increasing levels of emotional control
- enhancing sleep
- improving memory
- boosting immune system function

Every morning is a great opportunity to wake up and literally breathe yourself into a calm and positive start to your day.

How to shine with breathing

- Sit comfortably with your back straight, any-where that feels right for you (bed, chair, sofa, floor, grass).

- Let yourself settle and relax.

- Allow your eyes to close or soften your gaze, and rest one or both hands lightly on your stomach.

- Take a soft, slow, gentle, deep breath in (ideally through your nose), all the way down into your belly. There's no need to force it: just allow the breath to flow in smoothly.

- Pause briefly, then breathe out again, slowly and gently (ideally through your nose), simply allowing the breath to flow out smoothly.

- Feel the natural rise and fall of your belly as your breath easily flows in and out.

- Repeat this a few times, allowing yourself to settle and relax into the practice. You may find it helpful to imagine your breath smoothly inflating and deflating a big, blue balloon as you softly breathe in and out.

If you're new to breathwork, or are finding this works for you, we suggest you simply carry on doing this for a few minutes.

Once you've finished, allow your hands to rest lightly in your lap, letting your breath settle into its natural rhythm. Take a few moments to enjoy the sense of calm and clarity in your body and mind.

If, at any time, you feel uncomfortable or dizzy, just stop the practice and allow your breathing to settle and find its own rhythm.

If you want to progress further with your breathwork, one of our favourite morning breathing exercises is alternate nostril breathing (or *nadi shodhana* in Sanskrit). This yogic breathing practice helps balance the right and left sides of your brain. What's more, it also makes you feel awake and alert – rather like a cup of coffee, but without the caffeine.

Sit comfortably, ideally with your eyes closed. Gently close your right nostril by holding your right thumb over it. Inhale gently, slowly and naturally through your left nostril. Try not to force the breath – think smooth and steady, rather than forced and jagged.

○ At the end of your inhalation, close off your left nostril with your first finger, then lift your thumb and exhale gently and slowly through your right nostril.

○ Next, inhale gently, slowly and deeply through your right nostril, then close it off with your thumb once more, lift your finger and exhale through your left nostril.

○ Repeat this for between ten and twenty full cycles. If you find it easier than counting, set a timer on your phone for two or three minutes instead (but remember to put your phone on 'do not disturb' mode at the same time).

○ Feel the flow of the breath across your body, from one side to the other side, gently balancing and harmonising you.

○ Once you've finished, let your hands rest lightly in your lap as you quietly allow your breath to settle back into its own rhythm.

Savour the sense of spaciousness and peace you have created for yourself.

'I've experienced how drastically feelings of anxiety and overwhelm changed my breath, until it felt tight and painfully difficult, almost as if I couldn't breathe at times. This just made me feel more anxious and overwhelmed. Working with intentional breathing practices every morning has helped me break this vicious cycle. I find that a few minutes of alternate nostril breathing when I first wake up calms and rebalances me like nothing else. It's one practice I will always do, even if I only have a few minutes, as I know how wonderful it makes me feel. I also use it at moments throughout the day when I need a quick reset. I often teach my coaching clients breathing exercises and have seen the incredible difference this has made for them.'

– Kate

Candle gazing

'Look at how a single candle can both
defy and define the darkness.'

– Anne Frank, *The Diary of a Young Girl*

Lighting candles is a cornerstone of many celebrations, festivals and spiritual practices around the world. We use them to both celebrate life and commemorate loss.

Our eyes are naturally drawn to the flickering movement of fires and candles. This fascination with flames taps into something primal – our understanding of and respect for the power and importance of fire. Interestingly, the meditative trance state induced by candle gazing is one of the ways that modern hypnosis was discovered and developed in the nineteenth century.

In the yogic tradition, this practice of candle gazing is known as *trataka*, a Sanskrit word that literally means 'to gaze steadily'. According to the *Hatha Yoga Pradipika*, the classic fifteenth-century Sanskrit text on Hatha Yoga, candle gazing 'eradicates all eye diseases, fatigue, and sloth, and closes the doorway creating these problems'.

Candle gazing is an extremely simple and relaxing practice that generates a soothing state of peace and enhances your concentration.

What's more, a number of scientific studies have proven

the positive effects it brings to both the mind and the body. One study published in the *International Journal of Psychological and Behavioral Sciences* found that those who practise *trataka* had decreased levels of anxiety, depression and tension after just one month of regular practice. Another found a reduction in levels of the stress hormone cortisol, blood pressure and pulse rate – after just one thirty-minute session.

You don't have to practice *trataka* for half an hour as part of your S.H.I.N.E. routine to experience the benefits. As little as five minutes will start to make a difference.

How to shine with candle gazing

You can use any type of candle. You may prefer to use one made from natural wax, such as stearin, beeswax or soy wax. As smell has a powerful effect on our emotions, you might also choose a candle with a scent that evokes a positive state for you – however, this is optional.

Make sure you have matches or a lighter to hand. Place your candle on a low, stable surface – you could use your bedside table or a chest of drawers. The key thing is that, when sitting, the flame should be slightly below your eye level and approximately an arm's length away.

Remember to place the candle somewhere safe, away from draughts, bedding and curtains. Never leave a lit flame unattended, and don't forget to blow it out when you've finished.

- Light the candle each morning as soon as possible after you wake up.

- Sit comfortably with your back straight. Take a few gentle, deep breaths in and out. Allow yourself to relax and settle.

- Bring your attention to the candle and gaze at the living flame as it flickers and sways.

- Keep your full awareness on the candle flame. You may find that keeping the amount of other light in the room to a minimum helps.

- Try to keep your eyes relaxed and open as you continue to gaze at the flame. Resist the urge to blink for as long as you can.

- After a while, allow your eyes to close.

- See the image of the flame in your mind's eye and keep it in the centre of your awareness.

- When the image fades, open your eyes and focus back on the flame for a few moments.

- ☼ Close your eyes once more, again focusing on the mental image of the flame.

- ☼ Repeat a few more times until you feel ready to finish the practice.

'I have worked with this practice for many years, and find it particularly beneficial during the dark winter months. There is something magical about lighting a candle before daybreak and watching the flame as the light slowly changes with the sunrise. I've also found that lighting a meaningful candle helps set a more powerful intention to the practice. For me, this is a World Peace Flame candle, which I light as an offering for peace around the globe. The candle was created in 1999 when – for the first time in history – Flames of Peace were lit on five continents, flown across the oceans and united into one. This wonderful charity is dedicated to promoting world peace, and also funds other activities, including free eye care in India and solar lighting in Africa.'

– Toby

Free writing

'Writing is like breathing, it's possible
to learn to do it well, but the point
is to do it no matter what.'

– Julia Cameron, *The Right to Write*

Writing is a powerful form of self-expression. Anyone can do it, and it has nothing to do with being a good writer.

Free writing is just allowing your thoughts to flow out and on to the page. Doing this in the morning helps you tune in to your thoughts and feelings, and become more conscious as you start your day. It allows you to let go of things you may be holding on to from yesterday or from your dreams during the night. If you do it regularly, it has been shown to bring increased clarity, focus and creativity into your life.

Scans of brain activity show that journaling requires us to use the logical, analytical left side of the brain. While this part of the brain is occupied, it leaves the right-hand, creative, emotional side of your brain free to wander and make connections. This allows you to think more expansively, express your feelings and be creative.

In one study of over 2000 people, those who hand-wrote notes, ideas, thoughts and feelings daily were two and a half times more likely to experience relief from fear, anxiety and worry, and to have a more positive state of mind. They also had a greater sense of overall life satisfaction.

The evidence is clear – free writing, by hand, using paper and pen, can make a big difference to your well-being and mental health.

It can also improve your physical health, through helping you to process stressful life experiences more effectively. A review by the Royal College of Psychiatrists into a range of independent research studies shows numerous health benefits of expressive writing. These benefits include a stronger immune system, and reduced symptoms of a number of diseases such as asthma, arthritis, chronic pain and hypertension.

If you can make the time for it, a well-established method is 'Morning Pages', a practice outlined by Julia Cameron in her book *The Artist's Way*. She recommends three pages of longhand, stream-of-consciousness writing, done first thing in the morning. Think of it as clearing the decks and opening the sails before you voyage smoothly and unburdened into the day ahead.

You can use this time to clear your thoughts, bounce ideas off the page, express your hopes and dreams, and vent your emotions, allowing anything that comes into your head to come out of your pen and on to the page in any way you like. And you don't have to write three pages – just get started and see what flows ...

How to shine with free writing

Buy yourself a notebook and pen that you will enjoy using. It's important to write by hand on paper, as this is a key part of the practice. There's something special about the act of writing with a pen rather than typing or tapping on a device. It makes the whole experience more sensory, expressive and personal.

- Set some time aside when you will not be disturbed and start to write.

- Don't overthink – just start writing. There is no wrong way to do free writing. Free writing is about expressing yourself freely, not writing perfectly.

- If you don't feel like writing, write anyway. As the French saying goes, 'the appetite comes as you eat'.

- Write anything and everything that crosses your mind. Write what you are thinking. Write what you are feeling. Don't try to control or order what you write, or censor yourself in any way. Just let it flow.

- Write at least a full page (or three full pages for the complete 'Morning Pages' approach).

- It's not supposed to be smart or even make sense. And nothing is too silly, strange or stupid to be included. The important thing is to simply get it out on to the page.

- Write for your eyes only. Do not allow anyone else to read your free writing. You don't even need to reread what you've written. In fact, we recommend that you don't. It's important you don't start to critique it or become self-conscious about it.

- Write it down and let it go. Enjoy the day ahead feeling lighter, brighter and open to new possibilities.

'I have dyslexia, so learning to read and write didn't come easily to me as a child. My spelling is still terrible, but I don't let that stop me. Give yourself permission to let go of worrying about whether your spelling is right, your grammar perfect and your words appropriate – they're not meant to be. Simply savour the joyful release of free writing. You may well be surprised at what comes out and on to the page. I frequently am. And so are my many clients, who tell me how beneficial they have found this morning practice. One described it as "cleaning out the challenging thoughts so you leave them on the page, rather than carrying them into the day ahead". I love that.'

– Toby

Meditation

'It is meditation every morning that gives you
the wonderful capacity to stay patient and
forgiving no matter what the day brings.'

– Eknath Easwaran, *Words to Live By*

Meditation is an ancient practice that has many scientifically proven benefits. These include greater calm and contentment, clarity and concentration, and willpower and stamina.

There's nothing difficult or mysterious about meditation – anyone can do it. The intention is simply to bring about a deeper state of awareness by quietening the thinking mind and turning inwards.

The amount of research into the huge and varied benefits offered by meditation is growing year on year. One of the consistent results from meditation studies is an increase in quality of life reported by those who meditate. The key findings from a research review by the NIH (National Institutes of Health), the American medical research agency, indicate that:

- During meditation, your metabolism enters an even deeper state of rest than it does during sleep – for example, we consume 8 per cent less oxygen while we sleep, but as much as 20 per cent less when we are meditating. This means that meditation is a powerful way to help your body recover and sustain energy.

- Levels of the calming hormones melatonin and serotonin are increased by meditation, while levels of the stress hormone cortisol are reduced by it. What's more, meditation is the only activity proven to reduce blood lactate, a key marker of stress and anxiety.

- Meditators produce more of the 'youth hormone' DHEA as they age. This helps to decrease stress, heighten memory, preserve sexual function and control weight.

Research conducted by the Lazar Lab at Harvard University suggests that people who meditate regularly are actually changing their brains to be happier over the longer term. Meditation appears to wire in an increased ability to concentrate, manage emotions and feel compassion.

You can meditate in many different ways, including:

Meditating on a single point of focus

Concentrate completely on a single thing and shut out anything else, e.g. focusing fully on your breath, a candle flame (see candle gazing, page 43) or the chanting of a mantra (see page 133).

Observational meditation

Simply sit and notice any thoughts or emotions that come up, without judging and without getting caught up in thinking about them – like gently watching clouds appearing and disappearing as they float across an open sky. This is also known as mindfulness meditation (see page 59).

Guided meditation

Listen to someone lead you through a meditation process step by step.

As with anything new, it's best to explore different styles of meditation to find which one works best for you.

How to shine with meditation

If you've never meditated before, try this simple meditation on the natural breath.

☼ Sit comfortably with your back straight. Have your arms uncrossed and your hands lightly resting on your thighs or in your lap. Think regal, not rigid. This will help keep you alert yet relaxed. You may find that your bed is too soft to do this and that the floor or a chair is best.

○ Don't lie down, as it's far too easy to nod off again – this is a time of falling *awake* rather than falling asleep.

○ Set yourself a timer. If you are using your phone for this, put it on 'do not disturb' mode and face down so you don't get interrupted or distracted.

○ It doesn't matter how long you meditate for. Start with five minutes and gradually build up your time from there. You may come to discover that ten to fifteen minutes is a good length of time for you.

○ Allow yourself to relax. Close your eyes and bring your awareness to the rise and fall of your stomach with each inhalation and exhalation. (You may find it helpful to rest your hands lightly on your belly for a few breaths to help you with this.) Don't try to breathe in a special way. Just observe the movement of your stomach as your breath flows easily in and gently back out.

- Then shift your awareness to observing the movement of your breath in and out through the nostrils (or your mouth, if this is not possible for you). Notice the qualities of each breath, including how warm or cool it feels, how deep or shallow, how fast or slow. No need to judge or try to change anything; just to notice.

- It can help to count your breaths: 'One, breathing in. Two, breathing out. Three, breathing in. Four, breathing out.' Keep going until you get to ten, then begin again at one. Don't worry if you lose count or find your attention drifting – just start again at one and keep counting.

- To finish, take three deep breaths silently in and out, then stretch and gently open your eyes. Pause for a few moments and reflect on the experience and how you feel now, before moving on with your day.

'Being silent and sitting still doesn't come naturally to either of us. And those who've known us since childhood are astonished that not only are we able to sit quietly and meditate, but that we choose to do so. It's something that has surprised us both, too. It's taken practice, but the benefits have been huge, which is why meditation is one of the cornerstones of both of our morning routines. Don't worry if your mind wanders – this happens to us all. Just be gentle with yourself and simply bring your awareness back to the meditation. Some days, you might need to do this time after time after time. It's all part of the process. Remember: it is called a meditation "practice" – it's not about being a perfect meditator.'

– Kate & Toby

Mindfulness

'Mindfulness means being awake. It
means knowing what you are doing.'

– Jon Kabat-Zinn, *Wherever
You Go, There You Are*

In our busy lives, it's easy to rush through the day on autopilot. Too often we're living in the past or the future, dwelling on things that have happened or fixating on what might happen – so much so that we barely notice what's going on right *now*.

Mindfulness is the practice of paying more attention to the present moment – to your own thoughts and feelings and the world around you – without attachment or judgement. Young children and animals are naturally good at this; adults, often less so.

When we are truly present, it's not possible to either ruminate on the past or worry about the future. By being fully present, we improve our sense of calm, wellbeing and mental clarity, and find more enjoyment in our days.

Recent developments in neuroscience have shown that what we focus on and the way in which we focus our attention actually shapes the brain. This, in turn, shapes our experience of life. It is now widely accepted that our brains are not fixed. They have the ability to change and grow throughout our lives in response to new experiences, attitudes and actions. This is known as 'neuroplasticity'.

Numerous studies from many leading global research institutions, including the University of Oxford, show that a regular daily mindfulness practice helps cultivate concentration, creates a sense of inner peace and reduces both physical and psychological stress. What's more, neuroplasticity means that mindfulness actually alters the structure and function of the brain, making us more able to respond effectively to life's challenges.

If you haven't practised mindfulness before, a great place to start is by doing some of your regular morning activities (such as brushing your teeth, taking a shower or drinking your first cuppa) more mindfully.

You can also practise mindfulness in other ways, including meditation (see page 52).

How to shine with mindfulness

- Focus all your attention on a chosen morning activity, such as brushing your teeth. Be fully absorbed in the moment and all the fluctuating feelings and shifting sensations it brings.

☼ As you pick up your toothbrush, look at it as if you have never seen a toothbrush. As if you are seeing it for the first time. Really see it.

☼ Notice the sensations as you squeeze the toothpaste on to the brush. Notice the smell as you lift it towards your mouth. Notice how your hand knows exactly where to bring the brush to put it into your mouth. Notice how your mouth prepares to receive the brush and toothpaste.

☼ Then begin to brush your teeth, slowly, focusing on the different sensations, smells, sounds and tastes as you move the brush around your mouth. Keep focusing on these as you continue to brush.

☼ Lower your gaze or turn away from the mirror so you are not distracted by how you look while doing this.

☼ If your mind wanders, simply draw your attention back. If it keeps wandering, just keep bringing it back again. Be gentle with yourself. This is all part of the practice.

Remember, it's not about judging yourself or the activity – it's simply about training your mind to focus on the experience of the here and now.

'I often work with clients who are feeling overwhelmed and stressed by all the demands of their lives. Teaching them some basic morning mindfulness practices helps them find a few moments of calm as they rise, allowing the swirling thoughts in their minds to settle, so that they can think more clearly about the day ahead. Through practising mindfulness in the morning, they also find that they are more able to use these skills to reduce their stress at difficult moments in the day, such as in important meetings. This helps their days run more smoothly. They often tell me that, through practising mindfulness, they have also started to notice and pay attention to the many marvellous, underappreciated "small" things they would otherwise have missed – and feel happier as a result.'

– Kate

Structured journaling

'In the journal I do not just express
myself more openly than I could to
any person; I create myself.'

– Susan Sontag, *Reborn*

Journaling with a positive focus helps you start your day
with gratitude, clear intentions and focus.

This written practice differs from free writing (see
page 47) as it takes a more structured approach. If free
writing is simply letting yourself float downstream, then
structured journaling is rowing upriver with a clear
destination in mind. The aim is to reflect on and write
about a series of topics that help you enter your day with
a focused and positive mindset.

Structured journaling helps you feel more in control
of your life, and set and achieve clear goals. This, in
turn, reduces feelings of stress and anxiety, because it
increases your sense of self-efficacy. It will leave you with
more self-confidence and belief in your ability to cope
effectively with life's challenges.

Journaling has also been shown to create a more
internal locus of control. People with an internal locus of
control believe that they have control over the outcome
of events in their lives, rather than being at the mercy of

outside forces. So structured journaling in the morning will help you be more focused, determined and resilient in achieving what you want in that day.

Journaling also boosts your wellbeing and mental health, through creating a more positive mindset. Gratitude journaling in particular has been consistently shown to increase optimism and happiness, and reduce symptoms of depression. (See page 73 for more evidence on the power of developing a gratitude practice.)

As with the free writing practice, the process of writing by hand is important here, too. We know that taking a few minutes, in silence, to reflect and handwrite in your journal is a peaceful and powerful way to process, make sense of and structure your thoughts and feelings at the start of your day. As one of Toby's meditation teachers advises: 'Don't just think it, ink it.'

How to shine with structured journaling

Buy yourself a notebook and pen you will enjoy using, and set some time aside when you will not be disturbed – around ten minutes should be enough.

Work your way through the three areas below, writing down your reflections:

1. Today I am grateful for ...
    Write down three things you are grateful for.

2. Today I am looking forward to ...
    *This might be something you will get to do,
    people you will spend time with or talk to, or a
    time in the day that you are particularly looking
    forward to.*

3. Today I commit to ...
    *Write down three commitments you are making
    for today. These might be things you will do or
    achieve (see goal-setting page 106) or how you
    will be as you go through your day (see 'to-be' list,
    page 119).*

As you get used to this practice, you might
want to vary the questions you journal about.
Feel free to come up with your own questions,
as long as they create a positive mindset
and focus for the day ahead. Here are a few
more ideas:

*   Today I will use the following strengths of
    mine ...
*   Today I will look after myself by ...
*   Today I will help others by ...

'I have been using structured journaling as part of my morning routine for several years now. Before I started journaling, I barely wrote, and my handwriting had become really sloppy. I decided to make a deliberate effort to write neatly in my journal, in line with the belief that "how you do anything is how you do everything". I take great pride in my journal. I see it as a reflection of me, and it helps me to feel that I am starting the day with a sense of positive focus and order. It also enables me to be more appreciative of my life and more productive and successful. I doubt I'd have had the confidence or motivation to write this book without it.'

– Kate

Chapter 4

Happiness

'Ever since happiness heard your
name, it has been running the
streets trying to find you.'

– Hafiz

The scientific evidence is compelling – happiness really does matter. Happiness has been proven to have numerous benefits, including improved performance, health and relationships. What's more, it's contagious – people who are happier help those around them to feel happier, too.

Success is not the source of happiness; happiness is the source of success.

The six S.H.I.N.E. practices in this chapter will provide

you with a range of things you can do to bring delight into your morning. They will help you to move into your day with a smile on your face, feeling happy and uplifted.

- Hugging (page 68)
- Gratitude (page 73)
- Joy (page 78)
- Mirror work (page 82)
- Positive affirmations (page 86)
- Smiling (page 91)

Pick any of these – whichever appeals. If you're unsure where to start, gratitude and smiling are simple but powerful places to begin.

Hugging

'Everybody needs a hug. It
changes your metabolism.'

– Dr Leo Buscaglia,
Living, Loving and Learning

As humans, we are wired for connection and contact. Touch helps us develop, grow and thrive. Children and animals know this instinctively, with research showing they will even choose physical contact over food.

The renowned family therapist Virginia Satir said, 'We need four hugs a day for survival. We need eight hugs a day for maintenance. We need twelve hugs a day for growth.'

Current research backs this up. Starting the day with a hug sends a whole host of mood-lifting chemicals, such as oxytocin (the love hormone) and serotonin (the mood-stabilising hormone), whizzing around our bodies. These bring feelings of connection and belonging, and lift our mood.

There's increasing evidence that the giving and receiving of hugs improves wellbeing, boosts the immune system and has a stress-buffering effect. This means that regular hugs help keep you feeling upbeat and healthy, even on the most stressful of days.

Perhaps your days already start with a hug; perhaps they don't; perhaps it isn't something you have given much thought to. Whatever the case, it's really worth thinking about how you can consciously build hugging and physical contact into your morning routine. It doesn't matter who you hug (as long as they're a willing participant, of course): it could be a family member, your partner or a friend. And the great thing is that they will benefit from the hug too.

You don't even need someone else to do it – you can hug yourself or cuddle a pet, pillow or soft toy. Self-soothing is something we learn as children, but often forget as adults: that ability to cuddle and care for ourselves when in need, as we would a dear friend. Hugging yourself can release the same positive chemicals as sharing a hug with someone else, making you feel calm and loved.

How to shine with hugging

Let's start with hugging someone else. It's easy to assume you already know how to hug, but most of the hugs we give during the day (if, indeed, we give any) are brief and mechanical – so you won't see the full benefit.

Here are some key tips on how to hug someone close to you.

- First and foremost, make sure they are ready and willing to be hugged.

- Wrap your arms around them and hold them close.

- Hug warmly, but don't squeeze too tight or touch any sensitive areas without permission.

- Relax into the embrace and notice how your breathing starts to synchronise with theirs.

- Hold the embrace for at least twenty seconds. To gain maximum benefits, keep hugging for a minute or more.

There are also times when there's no one around to hug, so here's how to give yourself a really good hug.

- You can do this practice lying in bed, but we've found it works best for us done either sitting upright or standing. (You're also less likely to fall back to sleep if you aren't lying down!)

- First, open your arms wide, then wrap them around yourself. Relax your shoulders.

○ Now give yourself a nice big squeeze and hold for as long as you need to – sometimes a quick hug is enough; other times you might want something more gentle and long-lasting.

○ Notice which arm is on top. Then open your arms wide again and wrap them back around yourself, this time with the opposite arm on top.

○ Hold, or repeat, alternating the top arm, for as long as feels good.

○ If you're in any kind of pain or discomfort, crossing your arms in a self-hug can actually confuse the brain, minimising the negative sensations you're experiencing.

○ You might also find it soothing to gently stroke downwards on your upper arms, from shoulder to elbow, while they are lightly crossed. This has the magical effect of 'smoothing our feathers' and calming down the nervous system.

'I learned the power of this practice from a friend and fellow yoga teacher. She always ends her class by getting her students to throw their arms wide and then wrap them around themselves in a self-hug. This felt odd the first time I did it, but soon became a lovely and much-looked-forward-to way to thank myself for my practice. I taught this to Kate, who is often on her own at home, as her partner lives in another town. She tells me how much it has comforted her on mornings when she is missing him.'

– Toby

Gratitude

'Gratitude unlocks the fullness of life. It turns
what we have into enough, and more.'

– Melody Beattie

Practising gratitude is the act of consciously appreciating and giving thanks for all the good things in your life.

When you start your day with gratitude, you set yourself up to feel positive about the day ahead and to be resilient in dealing with the opportunities and challenges it brings.

Gratitude changes your perception of life, transforming a sense of lack into one of appreciation and acceptance. Research has shown that this has a positive effect on our feelings, beliefs and even on the cells within our bodies.

Every time you express or receive gratitude, dopamine (the 'pleasure chemical') releases in your brain, making you feel good. When you are feeling grateful, you can't also feel sad, worried or angry.

Numerous studies by leading psychologists consistently show that people who are more grateful are happier, less depressed and less stressed. They also tend to be more satisfied with their lives and relationships. In one study, people who kept a daily gratitude journal for two weeks experienced increased positive mood, greater optimism about the future, and better sleep.

It also helps your heart. A study by the UC San Diego School of Medicine found that patients who kept a daily gratitude journal had a reduced risk of heart disease after just eight weeks.

The more you practise gratitude, the more appreciative and thankful you will feel. As Professor Barbara Fredrickson says, 'Gratitude opens your heart and carries the urge to give back.' When we feel grateful, we tend to want to pay it forward – to reach out and do something good for someone else. This, in turn, strengthens our relationships.

What's more, the way we feel impacts on those around us, through a phenomenon called 'emotional contagion'. So practising gratitude is not just good for your own wellbeing, but for the wellbeing of those around you.

How to shine with gratitude

- Think about five things in your life that you are grateful for. Absolutely anything. They can be as big or as small as you like. It doesn't matter whether they would be meaningful to anyone else. The key thing is that thinking about them makes you feel grateful.

You can do this as a mental exercise – thinking about these five things – and counting them off on the fingers on one of your outstretched hands, almost as if you are holding these experiences in the palm of your hand.

You could choose to write them down in a journal (see structured journaling, page 62), in your diary, or on a sticky note that you put up somewhere you can see it throughout the day. This is a lovely way to remind yourself of what you are grateful for as you go through your day, amplifying the benefits of this practice.

Either way, try to be as specific as possible, to really evoke the feeling of gratitude in yourself. Rather than just being thankful for your partner, for example, elaborate on one specific thing you appreciate about them.

Really allow yourself to experience the feelings of gratitude and appreciation as you do this – this is not about simply making a list. To get the full benefits, you need to feel the feelings.

☼ Remember, this is about seeing the good things in your life as gifts, so that you don't take them for granted.

☼ Try to notice the unexpected or surprising, as these tend to elicit stronger feelings of appreciation.

☼ Consider these different gratitude prompts, so that you don't repeat the same things day after day. Repeating the same things every day tends to lessen the positive effects:

- Something that you can see, feel, hear, smell or taste right now – *e.g. birds singing outside, the sun shining, the coffee you're drinking, the comfy bed you just got out of.*
- Someone in your life, either now or in the past – *whom you love, who has helped you or whom you value highly. To add even more positive impact to this practice, you might want to send them a short text or note to express your gratitude by thanking them. There's evidence that this tends to have much more positive impact on the receiver than we imagine it will.*
- Something you do that helps you to feel positive about yourself and your life – *a*

hobby, a healthy habit or even one of your morning practices.

- Something that is coming up today – *an event, experience or opportunity that you are thankful for.*
- Something that happened yesterday – *either to you or that you witnessed happening to someone else, that you feel grateful for.*

'I used to spend a lot of time thinking about the things I didn't have; about what was missing or lacking in my life. It didn't make me very happy. Developing a daily gratitude practice shifted my entire outlook and this, in turn, started to change the way I felt about my life. It made me more content and much easier to be around – both for myself and those around me. Some days, it flows easily; other days, I have to really focus to find the things I feel grateful for. But once I have done this, I always feel much better about whatever lies ahead that day.

– Kate

Joy

'Follow your bliss and the universe will
open doors where there were only walls.'

– Joseph Campbell, *The Power of Myth*

If much of your day is spent doing things for other
people, this practice is about you making time at the
start of it to do something just for yourself.

When you are joyful, your whole body benefits. In
fact, research has found that joyful people have less
chance of experiencing a heart attack or catching a cold.
They also have lower cholesterol, more easily maintain a
healthy weight and experience less stress.

Perhaps it's not surprising that studies show joyful
people tend to live longer.

Beginning the morning with an activity that you love
helps get the day off to a great start. Do something that
makes your heart sing and your spirit soar.

Laughter Yoga uses fun movement and breathing
exercises to create prolonged, voluntary laughter. As
a Laughter Yoga leader, Toby often starts the day with
a good giggle by joining an early morning 'Telephone
Laughter Club'. It's not just great fun. A research project
involving 200 people working in IT showed that Laughter
Yoga decreased stress, reduced negative emotions by 27

per cent and boosted positive ones by 17 per cent, plus a whole host of other benefits. One of the reasons for this is that laughter – regardless of whether it's real or fake – releases endorphins (the 'pain-killing hormones') in our bodies. This gives you a natural high as you start the day.

For you, a joyful activity might be listening to a favourite song or an uplifting podcast, drawing, playing an instrument, or watching an inspiring video. The list is endless and highly individual. It's ideal if it's something you can do easily from the comfort of your own bed or in your own home. Then you can enjoy heading into your day knowing that whatever else happens, you've started your morning by doing something that makes you truly happy.

How to shine with joy

- Give yourself permission to simply enjoy yourself.

- It doesn't matter what you do. This is about you having a few minutes of pure, unadulterated pleasure and happiness. Do whatever brings you joy.

- Create your own 'Bliss List' to choose from. Here are a few ideas to get you started:

- Listen to the birds singing outside.
- Read a few pages of a book you love.
- Snuggle up with a loved one.
- Sing along to a favourite song.
- Eat something delicious.
- Open the window or back door and breathe in the morning air.
- Remember a happy memory.
- Do a crossword or puzzle.

☀ Remember, if you are using your phone to listen to or watch something, avoid getting sucked into checking your messages or updating social media. There will be plenty of time for that during the rest of your day.

'I may have been very late in learning to read (as a child with ADHD and dyslexia), but I've more than made up for it since because I love it. Reading brings me joy. Several years ago, I had a very busy and stressful full-time job, alongside which I was also building up my own theatre company. Looking at the towering pile of unread books I had bought or been given that year, I was shocked to realise that I'd pretty much stopped reading. I was simply too tired in the evening, and there didn't seem to be enough time in the day. So, the idea came to me to set my alarm fifteen minutes earlier each morning and to start the day by reading. It took time to adjust, but gradually I started setting it a little bit earlier to carve out even more time to rediscover my joy. The effects surprised me. Starting my day doing something I loved changed how I felt about and dealt with the rest of the day. I would fall asleep looking forward to my morning read, and wake up knowing I had something joyful to look forward to, regardless of how tough the rest of my day might be.'

– Toby

Mirror work

> 'Smile in the mirror. Do that every
> morning and you'll start to see a
> big difference in your life.'
>
> – Yoko Ono

Mirror work is a simple but powerful practice championed by Louise Hay in her bestselling book, *You Can
Heal Your Life*. It is not about vanity – it has nothing to do
with what you look like. It has everything to do with how
you see and feel about yourself.

Talking to yourself in the mirror is a great way to
use positive affirmations (see page 86) to build your self-
esteem and confidence. The more you use mirror work
to compliment and approve of yourself, the better you
will feel about yourself and your day.

A number of studies have explored the benefits of mirror work, and some of their findings are
shared below.

- Mirror work allows us to develop our emotional
  awareness. When we come face to face with our
  own reflection, we start to see our true selves
  behind the social masks we wear throughout the day.

- It helps us build a greater sense of self-acceptance. In order to change, we first need to learn acceptance. Mirror work creates an opportunity for us to notice the urge to criticise ourselves and move towards compassionate self-acceptance, acknowledging that no one is perfect, ourselves included. Research shows that looking in the mirror with the intention of being kind to yourself can reduce anxiety and self-criticism.

- It makes us less socially awkward. A study in the *Journal of Rational-Emotive & Cognitive-Behavior Therapy* found that people who stopped looking at themselves became increasing socially awkward and started to avoid socialising. We need to see ourselves reflected back to us. When we can accept and manage our own feelings, we are able to better connect with the emotional needs of others.

How to shine with mirror work

You can use any mirror – a bathroom mirror, full-length bedroom mirror or a good-sized hand mirror – just make sure it's big enough for you to see your whole face in.

Stand or sit and gaze into the mirror.

※ Look into your own eyes.

※ Look beyond your external appearance. We all have a tendency to focus on what we look like – that spot, those wrinkles, our noses, our body shape or size. Try instead to really *see* yourself through the windows of your eyes, without judgement.

※ Take a deep breath and say, either aloud or inwardly, '*I love and accept you, just the way you are.*'

※ If this is too challenging, try instead, '*I am willing to love and accept you, just the way you are.*'

※ Take another deep breath and repeat the affirmation, using your own name at the start. This makes it even more powerful. (For example, Kate would say, '*Kate, I love and accept you, just the way you are,*' or '*Kate, I am willing to love and accept you, just the way you are.*')

※ You may find it odd, awkward or embarrassing. Stick with it. Maintain eye contact. The more you practise, the easier it becomes.

○ Try to notice how you feel, and to notice any thoughts that arise without allowing yourself to get caught up in them.

○ You can stay with the process outlined above, or you might want to combine mirror work with your affirmations practice (see page 86), repeating your own affirmations to yourself in the mirror. The more, the merrier.

'A client of mine was experiencing anxiety and panic attacks. This was profoundly impacting their ability to work. Through practising mirror work, they became more aware of how critical they were in talking to themselves, and how this was feeding into their sense of imposter syndrome. Initially, this felt uncomfortable and stirred up a few emotions, but by sticking with this practice over a period of weeks, they learned to be far more accepting of and kinder to themselves. The panic attacks stopped. It also transformed how they felt about their work and life.'

– Toby

Positive affirmations

'The happiness of your life depends
upon the quality of your thoughts.'

– Marcus Aurelius

An affirmation is anything you choose to believe, think or say.

We make affirmations all the time, inside our heads (often called our 'inner voice') and when we speak.

Far too many of us start the day either worrying about something or criticising ourselves, perhaps without even realising we are doing this. Brain imaging reveals that when we practise negative self-talk, it has a similar effect on the brain as if someone else was saying those unkind words to us. These are *negative* affirmations, and they don't get our day off to a helpful or healthy start. For example, 'I hate mornings,' 'I feel rubbish,' 'I'm dreading that meeting today.'

Bestselling author and teacher Louise Hay was a pioneer in this field and championed the use of positive affirmations. For her, affirmations meant consciously choosing to think certain thoughts to create positive results. We think in words, so it makes sense that by changing the words we use, we can change our thoughts, which in turn changes how we feel.

Magnetic resonance imaging (MRI) scans show that activity in the parts of the brain involved in positively processing information about ourselves increases when people practise self-affirmations. Another study showed that we become more open-minded and less defensive. People who practise daily affirmations also have reduced levels of stress and worry.

So, choose to start the day with positive affirmations by saying things to yourself – either out loud or in your head – that are positive and encouraging. For example, 'Today is a bright new day.'

This will help you feel better in the moment, create positive feelings and energy about what's to come, and set yourself up for a less stressful day ahead.

How to shine with positive affirmations

○ Write down a list of between one and three positive affirmations about yourself and the day ahead.

○ Here are a few examples to get you going:

- 'I am awake, refreshed and full of energy.'
- 'Today is a good day, full of opportunities.'
- 'I can deal easily with today and all that it brings.'

○ You can get excellent books and recordings of positive affirmations, and these can be a good starting point. It is especially effective to create your own affirmations, as these will have most meaning to you.

○ To create your own powerful affirmations, follow these four steps, making sure your affirmations are positive, in the present tense, personal and persuasive:

1. Positive: Focus on what you want to happen, not what you don't want. For example, rather than saying, 'I won't lose my temper today,' a positive affirmation would be, 'I am calm and understanding, whatever challenges I face today.' Otherwise, you'll be reinforcing the negative situation you want to change.

2. Present tense: Phrase your affirmations as if they are already true now. For example, 'I am happy today,' rather than about what you want to be true in the future ('I want to be happy today'). If you affirm that something will be different in the future, then that's how you'll see it – as something that is always yet to happen. So, if mornings

are a struggle, you may wish to work with the affirmation, 'I rise and shine with ease. Today is a good day.'

3. Personal: State your affirmation in a way that feels relevant and meaningful for you. For example, when faced with a challenging day ahead, you could affirm, 'I am confident, calm and courageous, ready to face whatever the day brings.'

4. Persuasive: When saying your affirmations, it's vital to say them as if you truly believe them – as if they are already true for you. Don't worry if it feels odd or awkward at first. This is quite normal, especially if you're in the habit of being particularly critical of yourself, or you've been brought up not to boast. Over time, it will feel more natural. It's a case of 'fake it until you make it' here.

'Using positive affirmations has been life-changing for me. When I was experiencing a lot of anxiety, I began by using the simple affirmation: "I love and approve of myself and I am willing to change." I used it repeatedly, to replace the negative chatter that was going on inside my head. Gradually, I started to add others. I wrote them down as a list in my journal. I said them every morning and whenever I needed to throughout the day. As an added bonus, I found that if I woke up during the night, saying my positive affirmations would immediately put me into a relaxed state and I would drift off to sleep again – meaning I awoke in the mornings more refreshed. I regularly update the positive affirmations I use to reflect the things I want and need at this point in my life. It's so great to start the day saying kind and loving things to myself, and it doesn't matter if I say them out loud or in my head – the effect is the same.'

– Kate

Smiling

> 'Sometimes your joy is the source
> of your smile, but sometimes your
> smile is the source of your joy.'

— Thich Nhat Hanh, *Your True Home*

A simple smile has enough scientifically proven benefits to bring a big grin to your face. The act of smiling has been shown to:

- lower blood pressure
- decrease stress
- boost your immune system
- reduce pain
- improve relationships

How does it do this? Your body releases 'happy' chemicals – neurotransmitters, such as endorphins – when you smile. This is because the brain responds to the physical 'smiling' movements of the muscles in your face, and interprets them as happiness. Our bodies lead our brains.

It doesn't matter whether your smile is real or not. The body responds as if it is. This is the same principle as for Laughter Yoga (page 78). We 'simulate to stimulate'. In other words, we consciously choose to smile or laugh to trigger the associated inner happiness this brings.

Smiling is the ultimate three in one: it makes us look good, it feels good and it does us good!

How to shine with smiling

- Start each day with a smile. You can do this in bed, as soon as you open your eyes – just gaze up at the ceiling and smile.

- Hold the smile until you feel your face soften and relax into it. Keep smiling until it moves from a physical facial gesture to a warm feeling inside you – we call this the 'melt point'.

- Some days, you might wake up smiling or laughing anyway (lucky you!), and you can simply savour the moment.

- On other days, it might feel like the most strenuous exercise ever – but keep smiling until you feel a change, however subtle. It's a start.

- You might find it helpful to keep something that makes you smile by your bed or in your bedroom so that you can look at it as soon as you wake up. This could be a photo of a loved one, a beautiful bloom or a special gift from a friend; anything that will trigger a smile.

○ You could also try combining smiling with other morning practices. For example, in many yogic traditions it is considered important to adopt a soft, or half-smile, during your yoga practice (see page 171) and during meditation (see page 52).

'I first came across the idea of intentionally changing your emotional state through changing your physical stance when I did my NLP (neuro-linguistic programming) training. The self-development guru, Tony Robbins, puts it succinctly when he says: 'Motion leads emotion.' It's so simple once you realise it – but also really powerful. I can tend to be quite serious, especially when I have a lot to do. So sometimes I put a sticky note with a smiley face somewhere I will see it as I get ready, as a reminder to myself to smile. As soon as I do, I notice the difference in how it makes me feel.'

– Kate

Chapter 5

Intention

'Each decision we make, each action
we take, is born out of an intention.'

– Sharon Salzberg

Every moment of every day, you are faced with a multitude of choices. An intention is a commitment to a way of being, an action or a result. It involves making a choice. In making this choice, intention enables you to consciously create your day, rather than unconsciously letting your day create you.

Science tells us that people who spend time setting their intentions in the morning have a greater sense of clarity and purpose throughout their day. This helps them stay focused in the face of distractions and disruptions.

This section comprises six S.H.I.N.E. practices to empower you to start your day with a clear sense of what matters to you, how you want to use your time and what you want to achieve.

You can choose any of these practices. If you're unsure where to start, we suggest you try the alarm clock or mapping your day practices (if you don't already do these).

Alarm clock

'The breeze at dawn has secrets to
tell you. Don't go back to sleep.'

– Rumi

For many of us, the alarm going off is the first thing
we're aware of in the morning. Does it come as a welcome reminder or a rude awakening? The way you
use – and react to – your alarm are deeply engrained
habits that you probably don't even think about. Discover
how a few small changes to the way you use your alarm
can make a big difference.

By being more intentional in the way you set and
respond to your alarm, you can literally change the way
you enter your day.

Some people have a regular schedule and wake up
easily each morning without even needing an alarm.
Others have a less consistent pattern – sometimes
having to rise early, other days not. Regardless, it is
helpful and healthy for your body and mind to go to
sleep and wake up at reasonably regular times each
day. Most of us need to use an alarm, particularly on
days where we have work or family commitments to
attend to.

We each naturally have a form of internal body clock

called a 'circadian rhythm' – biological processes telling us when it's time to sleep and time to wake up.

Some of us are larks and find rising in the morning easy. Others are night owls and find waking early harder. This is known as your 'chronotype'. It sets the natural rhythm of when you prefer to sleep and wake, and when you are at your most alert and energised.

Our circadian rhythms are regulated by daylight. This is why 'early to bed, early to rise' has been shown to contribute to better sleep. The hormone melatonin, which regulates sleep, peaks at around 11 p.m., so staying up later than that can reduce your sleep quality.

There is an increasing body of evidence around the importance of sleep for our physical and mental health. So this really matters. If you are struggling to wake up when your alarm goes off in the mornings, it's worth considering going to bed a little earlier. You can train yourself to do this, regardless of whether you are a lark or an owl. Simple, but incredibly effective.

It is best to set your alarm for the time you need to be up, rather than repeatedly hitting the snooze button, as doing this disrupts your sleep and sets you up for a groggier day. By resisting the start of your day, you're teaching yourself it's all right not to follow through on your intentions.

And because the way you start your day sets the tone for the rest of it, here are some ideas on how to use your alarm to get you going in the most positive way possible.

How to shine with your alarm clock

- ☀ Use your alarm clock to stick to a regular schedule, as this is most helpful for your body's internal clock.

- ☀ Buy an actual alarm clock. That way, you can not only turn your phone off, but not even have it in the bedroom.

- ☀ Unless you are a very heavy sleeper, choose an alarm that's not too alarming. Many alarms ring with a jarring sound that creates tension as you first wake up. Find a soothing sound that doesn't jolt you out of sleep, or a piece of happy music you love that makes you smile or laugh as it rouses you (see smiling, page 91).

- ☀ If waking up is particularly challenging for you, place your alarm somewhere that's out of reach, so you have to get up to turn it off. The process of getting up starts you moving and helps create the energy you need to get going.

When your alarm sounds, try the five-second rule. Don't hit snooze – instead, count backwards from five to one and then get up. This countdown will help you push past feelings of hesitation and reluctance, and motivate you to get going in the morning.

Of course, you could choose to sleep with the curtains or blinds open – depending on the season and your schedule, not to mention your privacy – to allow the rising of the sun to naturally bring you out of sleep.

If your schedule or other circumstances don't allow for that, you might want to consider a sunrise alarm clock. These work like a personal sunrise – a gradually brightening light that gently rouses you from sleep, rather than jolting you awake. This helps you wake up naturally, leaving you energised for the day ahead. Some of our friends and clients sing the praises of these.

Or you could try a smart alarm clock that monitors how you are sleeping and wakes you at a suitable point in your sleep cycle, when you are already in a light sleep. This can help you escape that befuddled, still half-asleep feeling that tends to occur when your alarm wakes you suddenly from a deep sleep.

Above all, whatever alarm you choose, as you wake, remind yourself of the positive reasons for why you are waking up, and of the benefits of creating some time and space for yourself through your new morning routine. This will help build the motivation you need to rise and shine each and every day.

'It takes more effort to begin an action than to continue it – for example, it takes a lot more energy to launch a rocket than to sustain its flight into space. This is known as 'activation energy'. For some people, and on some days, waking up in the morning needs a lot of activation energy. An inspirational coach I know sets his alarm using the *Thunderbirds* theme: "Five … four … three … two … one … blast off!" This might not be everyone's choice, but it inspires him to get up smiling and motivated every day, ready to complete his morning routine.'

– Kate

Creative visualisation

'We always attract into our lives
whatever we think about most, believe
most strongly, expect on the deepest
level, and imagine most vividly.'

– Shakti Gawain, *Creative Visualization*

You already visualise, whether or not you realise it. This might be rerunning happy memories, or imagining the worst-case scenario about something yet to happen. It might even be finding your mind drifting off into a daydream during a quiet moment.

Creative visualisation involves imagining things as you want them to be, deliberately directing your mind towards seeing the positive outcomes you want.

Studies show that our brains don't know the difference between imagining something and actually doing it. That means that by doing visualisation (sometimes known as 'mental imagery' or 'mental rehearsal'), the mind believes that the result has already been achieved and sets us up to succeed. When you repeatedly visualise something, your brain believes it's possible. And this changes the way you think and act, so that you are more able to make it happen.

Put simply, visualising good things happening makes

us feel good and makes us more confident, motivated and able to achieve the things we want.

It's a tool that has long been used by elite athletes as part of their everyday training to help them perform at their best. There are also numerous amazing examples of injured sports champions and medal winners using visualisation to speed up their healing, reduce pain, overcome performance anxiety, and mentally rehearse sports skills and techniques at times when they were unable to train physically. In some cases, enabling them to be able to compete in World Championships and the Olympic Games not long after serious accidents. In addition, many well-known performers, entrepreneurs and leaders use it to focus and set themselves up for success at events, meetings, presentations and talks.

You can use creative visualisation to set yourself up to be your best self and have your best day: a day where you achieve great things and feel amazing. You may find it particularly powerful to imagine yourself achieving your goals for the day (see page 106) or to go through the plans you have set out for yourself while mapping your day (page 111) and visualising yourself achieving them all, happily and successfully.

How to shine with creative visualisation

- Sit somewhere comfortable, where you won't be disturbed.

- You may wish to set a timer for between three and five minutes.

- Breathe slowly, softly and deeply, and allow your eyes to close.

- Visualise yourself going through your day, from morning to night, successfully performing all your tasks with ease, confidence and enjoyment.

- Fill in as much detail as possible, using all your senses and emotions – see, hear, touch, taste, smell and feel your day unfolding – to help you bring your visualisation to life.

- If there is a particularly important or daunting task ahead, visualise yourself having already done it with ease and success. Imagine all the great feelings (such as pride, relief, excitement or self-confidence) that come from this.

☼   Finish by imagining yourself at the end of the day, looking back, having successfully accomplished all the things you set out to do. Enjoy how good this feels.

☼   If your mind wanders, simply bring it back to focus on what it is that you want to happen today.

☼   The key is to make the pictures in your mind as bright and vivid as you can. Really see yourself doing the things you want to do, and being the way you want to be. It's important to notice what you are doing, how you are doing it and how you feel while you are doing it. Pay attention to the small details – things like what you are wearing, your surroundings, the people you encounter and what they are saying. The more vividly you can imagine it happening, the better the results you will get.

☼   And remember that today, in your imagination, you are acting *ideally*. It doesn't matter if your life isn't much like this yet. Picture what you *want* to happen, and then see what *does* happen ...

'As Mark Twain reputedly said, "I've lived through some terrible things in my life, some of which actually happened." I used to waste so much time and energy imaging the worst-case scenarios about my day, and life in general. Then I turned this amazing skill I had for imagining the worst on its head, and started imagining the very best – and things really started to shift for me. It wasn't just that I felt better; great things started to happen more and more, just as I had visualised – things like writing and publishing this book. Creative visualisation is now a core element of my morning routine.'

– Toby

Goal-setting

'The way to achieve success is first
to have a definite, clear practical
ideal ⊤ a goal, an objective.'

– Aristotle

Have you ever ended your day thinking, *How on earth did
I get here? This isn't where I needed or wanted to be?* Of course
you have – most of us have at one time or another.

Starting your day without a clear idea of what you want
to achieve is a bit like jumping on the first bus that comes
along and expecting it to take you to the right place.

Setting goals for the day ahead helps focus your time
and energy, motivating you to take action. It also helps
you stay on the right track and avoid being distracted
from what you really want to do that day. There is an
extensive and well-established body of evidence to suggest that having goals helps us to perform better and
feel better about ourselves. Put simply, we need goals in
order to be at our best.

One reason for this is that human beings crave certainty – it makes us feel safe. Setting goals is a simple but
effective way to feel more in control. This is particularly
useful if you are feeling overwhelmed by everything you
think you have to do, and unsure of where to start.

Research also shows that setting challenging but attainable goals increases effort, focus and persistence. We try harder and don't give up so easily when we have a goal to achieve.

Clear, specific goals work better than vague ones. We need to know exactly what it is we are aiming for. We gain confidence from the achievement of goals, and that gives us the courage to set more.

Most importantly, it has also been proven that we're more likely to achieve our goals if we write them down on paper. For example, one recent study by the Dominican University of California showed that people who wrote out their goals in pen were 42 per cent more likely to achieve them. It's like making a contract or agreement with ourselves. Writing our goals down also means we can review them at the end of the day and create a record of what we've achieved.

How to shine with goal-setting

The most effective goals are known as S.M.A.R.T. goals – this means that they are Specific, Motivating, Achievable, Relevant and Time-bound.

- Specific: Be clear exactly what your goal is, because if you're not clear, how will you know when you've achieved it?

- **Motivating:** Focus on things that you really want, rather than what you *don't* want, e.g. 'I will be calm and clear in my meeting today,' rather than, 'I won't be stressed and flustered in my meeting today.'
- **Achievable:** Make sure it's something you *can* do. Don't set yourself up to fail by aiming for the impossible.
- **Relevant:** Pick goals that are genuinely important for you to achieve today. If they're not important to you, you're unlikely to have the will to achieve them.
- **Time-bound:** State when in the day you will do it, or how long you'll spend on it.

For example, if you have decided that you will benefit from drinking more water (see water, page 145), your S.M.A.R.T. goal might be to 'drink six glasses of water by the end of the day'.

Set yourself one or more S.M.A.R.T. goals in one or more of these three areas, ideally at least one goal per area:

- Your wellness – e.g. exercise, sleep, healthy eating, 'me' time, doing things you love.
- Your work – e.g. things you want to achieve

at work or at home, or other tasks you need to get done.

- Your relationships – e.g. nurturing and improving relationships with family, friends, colleagues, neighbours or in other communities.

Think about how much time you will allow for each of these activities.

Remember to write down or record each goal somewhere you can see it and review it at the end of the day.

'When I am coaching someone, I always recommend that they don't set too many goals at any one time. It is much better to focus on a few things that you are really committed to doing, than on a long wish list you are unlikely to remember or have time for. When you set yourself a goal and do not achieve it, it can erode your trust in yourself – so be realistic and take it step by step. Once you have achieved your first goal, you can always set yourself something a bit more ambitious the next day. I also find it particularly helpful to set goals for the things I might otherwise avoid. By writing a goal in my journal, I am making the commitment to myself to tackle this thing today. And I usually find that I feel a lot better for having done so!'

– Kate

Mapping your day

'Either you run the day or the day runs you.'

– Jim Rohn

In our busy lives, it's common to rush through the day, overwhelmed by everything we have to do. Sometimes, we get to the end of the day wondering where the time went.

There's great power in deciding when and where you are going to do something; in making conscious choices about how you will use your time to do the things you need to do *and* the things you want to do. Both are important to your success and wellbeing.

Mapping your day is about prioritising the tasks and opportunities ahead of you. It's also about scheduling your day in a format that works for you. We are more likely to follow through on our intentions if we commit to where and when we will do certain things.

Think of this practice as creating a bespoke map to guide you through your day.

This practice is even more useful if you have the freedom to decide how you spend your time, rather than having a prescribed work schedule – for example, if you run your own business or are working from home, with the potential for lots of distractions.

Our brains work best when given clear goals (see page 106) to focus on for short periods of time (ideally no more than an hour), punctuated by short periods of rest and recovery. Think about mapping your day as planning out a series of sprints, with breaks in between, rather than a marathon.

If you are working at home, you might also want to build in clear boundary markers – points of transition from home to work and work to home. This is of key importance to our wellbeing and requires conscious thought and action. You'll find more on this in Chapter 9.

How to shine with mapping your day

☼   Before checking your messages or turning on your computer, take some time and decide what will make this day successful.

- List the jobs/tasks that absolutely must be done today (see goal-setting page 106).
- List the people you need to contact or connect with today.
- List at least one thing you will do today that will make you feel happy (see Joy, page 78). This'll help you get through the other things better.

○ Be realistic about what it is possible for you to achieve in your day. Don't set yourself up to fail.

○ Now, map out your day: create a schedule showing when in the day you will do each activity. You might find it helpful to divide your day into chunks of time, or you could use a diary or planner – choose whatever works best for you. What is important is to allocate a specific time for each task or activity, and to record your plan somewhere you can see it and refer back to it during the day, to help you keep on track.

○ Make sure you build in preparation time to your schedule, so you don't underestimate how long things will take.

○ If your entire list does not fit into your day, you're trying to do too much and need to reprioritise.

○ Remember to allow yourself time for breaks, food and drinks during the day – our bodies and brains don't operate well if we keep working without stopping.

- If you want more help in developing ways to help you map your day and manage your time effectively, you might find it helpful to look into bullet journaling, a highly structured method of planning ahead and staying on top of daily tasks.

- Another useful tool is the Pomodoro Technique developed by Francesco Cirillo, which helps you to divide tasks into structured time chunks, with brief periods of rest and recovery in between.

'A great tip our dad, Peter, taught us is "worst job, first job". In other words, do whichever job or task is hardest or least appealing first in the day, when you have most mental energy. Research shows that our willpower has a daily cap and tends to decrease as we move through the day. So it's most helpful to get the tough thing out of the way (as opposed to worrying about it and putting it off). Not only will it feel great to have mastered the monster, it will also give you more energy and motivation to get the other things done.'

– Kate & Toby

Mindset

'The mind is everything. What
you think you become.'

– Buddha

Your mindset is essentially your outlook on life: it affects how you think, feel and act. This plays a key part in how you cope with life's challenges and opportunities.

Our brains are wired for survival, which means they're constantly on the lookout for threats. This keeps us alert and helps us avoid potential danger, but the downside is that it can all too easily create a negative mindset where you are mainly focusing on problems and what might go wrong. And with this mindset, there's every chance your day won't go that well.

What's more, every time we think something, the pathway of this thought is reinforced in the brain, so over time, this pattern of thinking happens more easily. The more we focus on issues and dangers, the more alert to them we become. It's a vicious cycle.

The good news is that you can change your mindset through retraining yourself to focus more on the positives rather than the negatives; to see the opportunities rather than the threats; to reflect on your strengths rather than your weaknesses. This is about being conscious and intentional in your outlook on the day ahead.

In a wide range of research studies, a positive mindset has been shown to relate to:

- improved job performance
- greater entrepreneurial success
- higher levels of job satisfaction
- increased wellbeing

The questions we ask ourselves have a powerful influence on our thinking. Therefore, one of the best ways to cultivate a positive mindset is by answering a few simple questions as you start your day: questions that encourage positivity, to help you rise and shine, whatever the day brings.

How to shine with your mindset

☼ Allow yourself a few moments to pause and consider the following questions:

- What is something I am looking forward to today?
- How can I make a positive difference today?
- Which of my strengths can I use today?
- How can I make myself or someone else happy today?

○ Take a bit of time to tune in with yourself and reflect. You may want to answer these questions silently in your head, say your responses out loud as if talking with someone, or jot them down on paper. Play around to see what feels right for you.

○ Where possible, try to find different answers to the questions each time you use this practice, so you are not just going through the motions. It's important to keep it fresh, thoughtful and meaningful.

○ We recommend that you structure your answers as sentences, because this creates greater focus on and commitment to them. For example, you might say or write, 'Something I am looking forward to today is talking to my best friend,' rather than just 'Talking to my best friend'.

○ If you have written your answers down, you might find it helpful to stick them up somewhere, as positive reminders to nudge you throughout the day.

○ Of course, you don't have to limit yourself to these questions. Feel free to add others that help you build a positive mindset for the day ahead.

'It can be a real wake-up call when you realise how much your negative mindset is impacting on your day. Both of us have been through tough times, such as coping with significant illness, losing a job or ending a marriage. During these hard times, we tended to expect the worst from the day ahead – and invariably found it. It became a habit: an unhelpful one. But by consciously developing a positive mindset, and starting to shift our focus from one of great fear to one of good fortune, we discovered that our resilience grew and our days became brighter. A simple but effective mind hack we've found is to change the words "got to" to "get to". So, when we catch ourselves saying, "Today I've got to go to two meetings . . . ", we change it to "Today I *get* to go to two meetings . . . " The shift in feeling and motivation is immediate.'

– Kate & Toby

'To-be' list

'We are "human beings"
not "human doings".'

– John Bradshaw, *Healing the
Shame that Binds You*

As the saying goes, 'It ain't what you do, it's the way that you do it.' Many of us start our days thinking about the things we need to get done, but rarely stop to think about how we need to 'be' while doing them.

It's a subtle but important distinction.

The way you are *being* (not just what you are *doing*) has a big impact on the success of your day. For example, you can rush through *doing* lots while *being* distracted, grumpy and resentful. That is unlikely to deliver great results or leave you feeling happy about your day.

Alternatively, you can choose to be more conscious and aware not only of what you are doing, but also how you are being while doing it.

If you want to have a great day, achieve a lot and feel good, take a moment to reflect each morning on how you need to *be* in order to make this happen.

This is about shifting your focus to who and how you are, and choosing to show up with intention in the things you do. The more you embody a way of being, the more you start to actually feel it, and the easier it becomes. It's a virtuous cycle of positive change.

You might even find that reflecting on your 'to-be' list changes your to-do list, as you start to reflect on what really matters to you today.

How to shine with your 'to-be' list

- Ask yourself, 'How do I want and need to be in order to succeed in achieving my goals today?' Write down all the positive qualities you will need during the day ahead – this is your 'to-be' list.

- You may not have stopped to think about this before. If you need a little bit of help identifying some positive qualities, you could choose from the list in the table below. This is not an exhaustive list, so don't feel constrained by it. Feel free to add in other qualities or create your own list.

assertive	creative	flexible	kind
calm	curious	focused	loving
compassionate	determined	forgiving	open-minded
composed	empathetic	gentle	patient
confident	engaging	grateful	positive
courageous	energetic	happy	supportive

○ Pick up to three qualities that feel most important for you today, or choose the qualities you need for specific activities. If you have lots to do today, perhaps you want to be calm, focused and productive. If you have an important meeting coming up, maybe you want to be confident, composed and engaging. And if you have had a busy week and are tired, perhaps you need to be gentle, compassionate and kind to yourself.

○ Write your chosen qualities on a sticky note and place it somewhere you will see it throughout your day, or write them on a piece of paper to carry in your bag or pocket and refer to when helpful. You could even add reminders to your diary or phone. Remember that this is how you are *choosing* to be today.

☼ Then think about what you will actually *do* to embody each quality. For example, how will you be 'courageous'? By picking up the phone and making that call you have been putting off? By preparing the things you will say in the meeting to assert your point of view? By saying 'no' to the request from that person who is always asking you for favours?

'I had never practised this before Kate and I came together to write this book. That's one of the joys of collaborating: discovering new tools that help you to transform your day by transforming yourself. I was so focused on *what* I needed to get done, it had never occurred to me that I could also focus on *who* and *how* I wanted to be while doing it. What a difference! A "to-be" list is now one of my key morning practices. So many clients experience a similar "Aha!" moment when I share this practice with them.'

– Toby

Chapter 6

Nourishment

'If I am not good to myself, how can I
expect anyone else to be good to me?'

– Maya Angelou

It can be easy to get caught up in looking after everyone and everything else, but neglecting to take care of yourself. Nourishment is central to your wellbeing, and it's not just about the food you put into your body.

In order to thrive, you need to nourish all aspects of yourself.

Offered here are six S.H.I.N.E. practices you can use to feed your mind, body and soul, helping you to flourish. So, start your day by giving yourself the sustenance you need.

Pick any one or more of these practices. If you don't already do these, we recommend the water and breakfast practices to get you started.

Breakfast

'Breakfast is always the time for something
juicy, sweet and fresh – it just feels
like the right way to open the day.'

– Yotam Ottolenghi, *Simple*

Breakfast is important: when you eat, what you eat and how you eat it.

What we put into our bodies has a big impact on how well we function and how good we feel. Our bodies and minds need the right kind of fuel to stay healthy, work effectively and maintain good energy levels throughout the day.

Enjoying a healthy breakfast is a great opportunity to start the day by respecting and nurturing your body with something nutritious. Dozens of studies from as far back as the 1950s have consistently shown that children who eat breakfast perform better academically than those who don't. It's no different for us adults.

While the average person's brain represents just 2 per cent of their total body weight, it accounts for 20 per cent of their body's energy use. And our brains are powered purely by the glucose our bodies produce from digesting the food we eat. So we literally need to feed our minds in order to be able to think.

Without breakfast, you are running on empty – it's like trying to use your phone when it has no power left. Everyone is different, but we recommend always eating something within two hours of waking.

On working days, or particularly busy days, some of us might be tempted to skip breakfast to try and 'save time'. But breakfast recharges your batteries, which helps you concentrate on your work and gives you the energy and enthusiasm you need to get things done.

When you wake up, the blood sugar your body needs to make your muscles and brain work is usually low. When our blood sugar levels are low, it not only affects our ability to think, it also negatively affects our mood. You've no doubt experienced yourself and others being 'hangry' at times.

Eating breakfast boosts our mood. One study conducted by the the School of Psychological Science at the University of Bristol found that people who ate breakfast had a more positive mood, performed better on a memory task and felt calmer than those who had nothing to eat.

What's more, research shows that when people are in a better mood, they tend to choose healthier things to eat. So by eating a healthy breakfast, you are also setting yourself up to make better food choices in the day ahead. Eating breakfast also kick-starts your metabolism, helping you burn calories throughout the day.

And, let's face it, any meal is also far more than just fuel for our bodies. The food we choose to eat can give us enormous pleasure and stimulate many positive emotions through the associations it brings. A breakfast that feeds both body and soul is a wonderfully nourishing way to start the day.

How to shine with breakfast

There are many differing schools of thought around what makes a healthy diet. Most agree that it's best to eat fresh, natural produce and avoid excessive amounts of fat, sugar and salt, as well as heavily processed food. The general advice from health experts is to eat a well-balanced breakfast: one that delivers its energy slowly over the course of the morning.

- Think about what you enjoy eating and what works best for you. We are all different, and our needs will change as our lives change.

- To make breakfast more pleasurable, select something you will look forward to having as your first meal of the day. Enjoy the experience of choosing or making something delicious to eat. Some people like to prepare it the night before, while others enjoy making their breakfast as part of their morning routine. Do whichever is best for you.

○ If you aren't in the habit of having breakfast, start small by introducing a piece of fruit or something else light. You should find that, after a few days, your morning appetite grows.

○ Variety is the spice of life. Make your breakfast interesting by regularly trying something new.

○ Take time to sit down and enjoy the process of eating. Try not to rush or eat on the go. You could even use it as a mindfulness practice (see page 58).

'I used to make myself eat pretty much as soon as I woke up, but I realised this wasn't helping me – it got my day off to the wrong start and just made me feel worse. Remember, there is no "right" way to do this. Different people's bodies need different things, and they also need to eat at different times. My husband feels best if he eats almost as soon as he wakes up, whereas I now prefer to have a cup of tea as I go through my morning practices, then a healthy breakfast afterwards.'

– Toby

Learning

'Learn as if you were to live forever.'

– Mahatma Gandhi

Think of this practice as feeding your brain the mental breakfast it needs to get the day off to a great start.

We can all keep learning, whatever age we are, and there are many good reasons for doing so. The more we engage in learning, the easier we find it. Our brains change and grow throughout our lives. If we feed ourselves a varied, enjoyable and stimulating mental diet, we're giving our brains the best chance to stay fit, flexible and focused.

A number of studies into the benefits of lifelong learning show it increases resilience and mental health. This includes a study conducted by the Oxford Review of Education, which discovered that learning throughout life:

- gives you a sense of accomplishment and builds your confidence
- makes you feel happier and more fulfilled
- helps you become more curious, creative and adaptable to change

Furthermore, it has been found that learning keeps your brain healthy, creating new connections between cells that can help stave off dementia.

The morning is a particularly good time to learn, as your mind is usually alert after a refreshing night's sleep. Even if you tend to wake up feeling groggy, spending a bit of time gently learning something can be a good way to switch on your brain and sharpen your focus for the day ahead.

Sometimes, learning is about deepening an existing skill or rediscovering a dormant passion. At other times, it's about learning something totally new. Either way, it doesn't have to be about becoming an expert or being perfect. Try to see this as something you do simply for the challenge and enjoyment of growing, discovering and improving.

How to shine with learning

- Try to focus on your passions rather than your latest work-related project. Your brain will be fed more than enough of that during the day.

- You might want to acquire a new skill or hone your talents, for instance, learning a language or playing a musical instrument.

- Experiment to find the methods of learning that suit you best. You could try a whole range of things, including: reading, listening to audiobooks or podcasts, watching videos, taking a course, or simply just giving things a go to learn from the experience.

- Have enough challenge in the activity to ensure you are learning, but remember to keep it enjoyable. This is about feeding your mind, not putting pressure on yourself.

- Build some variety into your learning. We learn best when things are novel and engaging. Try not to get stuck in a rut.

- You might also find it motivating to set yourself some goals around your learning (see page 129).

'We grew up with a great role model for lifelong learning in our granny, Lisi. At the age of eighty-two, she decided to learn Italian, first to GCSE and then to A-level standard. She was still learning advanced Italian at ninety-two. I recently decided to learn

Spanish – partly because I love going to Spain, but also because there's so much evidence now of how learning languages (and musical instruments) helps keep our brains young and healthy. I used an app and dedicated ten minutes to it each morning. I was amazed to rediscover the joy I got from learning a language; something I had not done since leaving school more than thirty years ago.'

– Kate

Mantra

'Chanting is a way of getting in touch with
yourself. It's an opening of the heart and
letting go of the mind and thoughts . . . it's
a way of being present in the moment.'

– Krishna Das

Sound has a profound effect on us, physically, mentally
and emotionally.

We all know the joy of hearing a favourite song or the
upset felt at the cries of a loved one in pain. The use of
mantra taps into the positive power of these neurolog-
ical and psychological effects.

The word 'mantra' is formed from two Sanskrit words.
The first, *manas*, means 'mind' and the second, *trai*, means 'to
protect' or 'to make free'. So, the literal meaning of mantra is
something that protects or frees us from the mind.

At its most basic level, a mantra is simply a series
of sounds repeated – usually chanted or sung – a
number of times.

A recent study on the mantra effect published in the
journal *Brain and Behavior* showed that silently repeating
a single word to yourself quietens the areas of the brain
responsible for self-criticism, dwelling on the past and
worrying about the future.

Most traditional mantras are in the ancient Indian language of Sanskrit, and are said or chanted 108 times, using a string of beads, known as a *mala*, to count with. Each mantra is associated with different qualities or ways of being that we wish to bring into our world.

Whatever mantra you choose to work with, there are many other well-documented benefits, such as:

- a clearer focus
- reduction in stress
- more positive thinking
- increased immune function
- lower blood pressure

All very helpful and important things when dealing with the challenges and opportunities you may face during your day.

How to shine with mantras

You can choose any word or phrase to use as a mantra, as long as it has meaningful and positive connotations for you.

A lovely traditional Sanskrit mantra to begin with is: '*Om shanti shanti shanti*' (pronounced 'ah-oh-mm shan-tee shan-tee shan-tee-ee'). In Sanskrit this means 'Peace, peace, peace for all living beings'.

If this feels a bit of a leap, you could simply use the English translation, or something similar. Whatever feels right for you.

- You can sit or stand, either with your eyes closed or your gaze lowered.

- Relax and allow your breathing to become soft, slow and gentle.

- Begin to repeat your chosen mantra aloud, over and over again.

- Don't worry about getting it right or trying to make a beautiful noise. The important thing is to just immerse yourself in the sound of the mantra. Really savour the feel and taste of it as you speak it.

- If you feel really uncomfortable saying the mantra out loud, try saying it to yourself in your head. This will still have a positive effect.

- Continue for a few minutes – you could start with sixty seconds and build up.

☼ Any time you find your mind wandering, gently bring it back to the mantra. Don't judge or criticise yourself. Just refocus on the mantra.

☼ Finish by sending thoughts of peace to anyone you feel would benefit from them.

☼ You can find recordings and videos of this and many other mantras online. You may find it helpful to start by listening and chanting along.

'My mind is often like a jumping monkey – swinging from thought to bright idea, bright idea to thought, with a few suggestions for the to-do list along the way. I find that using a mantra during my meditation practice really helps by giving me something active to focus on. Sometimes I'll say the mantra aloud, other times I'll simply repeat it silently to myself. I have a friend who prefers to write her mantra down over and over – a positive take on giving yourself lines! Experiment with which method feels right for you.'

– Toby

Nature

'All my life through, the new sights of nature made me rejoice like a child.'

– Marie Curie

In our busy daily lives, it's all too easy to forget that we are part of the natural world and all its wonders.

You were not designed to exist mainly indoors, sitting under artificial lights and breathing in recirculated air. You need to fill your lungs with fresh air and enjoy sunlight on your skin to feel healthy (see sunlight, page 141).

Like us, you probably find spending time outside helps free your mind so you can think more clearly and be more creative. The Japanese call this practice '*shinrin yoku*', or 'forest bathing', and regard it as a cornerstone of wellbeing and preventative medicine.

There is an increasing body of evidence showing that connecting with nature has significant and wide-ranging benefits, including:

- boosting energy levels
- making you feel more alive
- decreasing stress levels
- improving creative problem-solving ability

- enhancing life satisfaction
- improving overall mental wellbeing

There's also evidence that time spent outside reduces the risk of developing serious health conditions such as type 2 diabetes, heart disease and high blood pressure.

One study by the University of Exeter Medical School showed that the benefits were true for just about every group you could think of: young and old, wealthy and poor, those with long-term illnesses and disabilities, and those living in rural and urban areas.

The researchers found the key factor was spending at least two hours in nature per week. Interestingly, this doesn't need to be all in one go; a series of shorter daily visits will offer the same benefits.

So, it could simply be a matter of spending around seventeen minutes outside in nature each day. The message is clear: getting out into nature is good for us all. And it doesn't have to be while doing physical exercise, you could just sit outside on a bench and observe the beauty of the world around you. Whatever feels most natural.

How to shine with nature

- ☼ Go outside each morning, even if it's just a few steps outside your back door. Take a deep breath and look around you. What can you see? What can you hear? What can you smell?

If it's warm enough, try standing barefoot on the grass or ground for a few moments. It can be powerful to imagine yourself growing roots down into the centre of the earth and plugging yourself back in to the energy of nature, as if you were recharging your batteries.

Remind yourself that whatever business or busy-ness you may have going on in your life, nature will carry on doing its own thing. And you are part of nature, connected to everyone and everything.

If you don't have a garden or outside space, open a window to bring in some fresh air. Look up at the sky and listen to the birds singing.

Even better, go for a morning walk and take in the natural world around you. Maybe you could build a brief stroll past some greenery, even through a park or by some water, into your morning journey to wherever you need to be.

☀ You could try practising mindfulness (see page 58) as you walk, by really focusing on the sights, sounds and smells you are experiencing. This is a calming and connecting way to start to the day.

'We both inherited a love of nature and being outside from our mum, Yvonne. She is a wonderful (and prize-winning) gardener who loves nothing better than being outdoors with her plants or feeding the birds, in all weather. She would be the first to tell you how beneficial spending time in nature has been for her physical, mental and emotional health. It's one of the simplest and yet most effective lessons any of us can learn. Thanks, Mum.'

– Kate & Toby

Sunlight

'Turn your face to the sun and the
shadows fall behind you.'

– Maori proverb

There are few things more glorious than waking up to a room glowing with golden sunlight.

The sun is the star at the centre of our solar system. It is by far the most important source of energy for life on earth. Without it, none of us would be here.

What's more, exposure to natural light does all sorts of good things for you, both mentally and physically. Getting the right amount of sunlight on your skin is essential for your body to make vitamin D. A lack of vitamin D in the body can lead to tiredness, and adversely affect your immune system, bones, teeth and muscles.

A study by the University of Edinburgh found that sunlight on the skin even helps lower blood pressure, reducing the risk of heart attack and stroke. Sunlight also stimulates production of the hormone serotonin. This results in a brighter mood and a calm yet focused outlook, leading to higher levels of productivity.

Research shows that the amount of sunlight you receive during the day has a direct impact on how much sleep you get at night. Direct sunlight, especially early in the morning for at least half an hour, has the most beneficial effect on your quality of sleep. Artificial lighting has little to no effect, unless you use a special SAD lamp, which you will find more information about below.

All in all, plenty of reasons to let the sunshine in.

How to shine with sunlight

- When the seasons allow, wake up and open your blinds or curtains before turning on the lights, to allow the natural light to enter. You may even choose to sleep with your windows uncovered so you wake up naturally with the morning sun.

- If the timing allows, watch the sun rising. Sunrise is a magical time – a reawakening of the planet and the dawn of a bright new day.

- If you can, get outside into the sunlight. Turn to enjoy the warmth of the morning sun on your face and body. Imagine yourself being filled with the sun's golden light, boosting your energy for the day ahead.

- A word of caution – we now know the risks of excessive exposure to strong sunlight. So, know your own skin, and if you have any concerns, seek medical advice.

○ At times of the year when sunlight is limited, some people find that light therapy, using a special lamp called a 'light box', can be really beneficial. These are designed to treat SAD (seasonal affective disorder – in essence, low mood caused by lack of sunlight), so they are also known as 'SAD lamps'. They come in various designs, including bedside and desk lamps, and produce a very bright, full-spectrum light that simulates the sunlight missing in winter. You turn on the lamp and sit by it for around thirty minutes to an hour each morning – so you could have it on in your room as you carry out other elements of your morning routine.

'Having a dog to walk certainly means I get outside in nature every morning, whatever the weather. And when I can, I love to take my morning yoga practice outside, to maximise the benefits by combining it with being in nature and under the sun. Traditionally, the yogic sun salutation (Surya Namaskara in Sanskrit) is performed outside, to greet and show appreciation for the rising sun. If you get the opportunity to do this, I'd highly recommend it.'

– Toby

Water

'Water is the driving force of all nature.'

– Leonardo da Vinci

Water is essential to life. Around 70 per cent of your body is made up of the stuff, with all your cells, organs, and tissues needing water to function healthily.

You lose water as you sleep, through respiration and perspiration. Exactly how much you lose varies, according to the temperature of the room, how warm your bed-covers are and how much you naturally sweat – but it could be as much as half a litre every night.

What's more, assuming you've slept through the night, you've probably gone without drinking anything for around eight hours.

This means you are very likely to be dehydrated when you wake up. You are thirsty, even if you don't feel it.

Proper hydration is key to staying in tip-top cognitive shape. Research published by the *Journal of the American College of Nutrition* indicates that not drinking enough water can negatively impact your focus, alertness, and short-term memory. Even a small drop in hydration – as little as 1–3 per cent – has a negative impact. In other words, when you're not properly hydrated, you will feel drained and unable to think clearly, and you will experience mood fluctuations. Not a great way to start the day.

Drinking water first thing in the morning rehydrates and wakes you up, helping you function at your best.

It also keeps you healthy by:

- encouraging the production of blood cells
- balancing your lymphatic system, which helps to fight infections
- cleansing your body of toxins
- boosting your metabolism

Drinking a glass of water thirty minutes to an hour before your first cup of tea or coffee of the day is best, because the caffeine in your cuppa will actually dehydrate you further. This practice also sets up the positive and healthy habit of drinking more water throughout the rest of your day.

It's an incredibly simple but effective habit ... so why not dive into it?

How to shine with water

☼ Aim to drink at least a glass of water when you wake.

○ It is best to avoid drinking really cold water first thing in the morning, as this can be a shock to the system – room temperature or warm water is better.

○ Fill a glass or water bottle with water before you go to bed. Place the cup or bottle beside your bed so that you can see and reach for it first thing in the morning.

○ If you prefer to drink warm water, fill an insulated cup or bottle before going to bed. This can be particularly comforting in colder weather.

○ You could try adding a slice of fresh ginger, orange, lemon, lime or mint to your water for some extra flavour and zing.

'I was not in the habit of drinking water in the mornings until a couple of years ago, when a physio I was seeing for a back problem recommended the practice to me. As soon as I started doing it, I noticed the positive effect it had on my mood and energy. I use a small metal water bottle, which I fill every night before I go to bed. It's great as it doesn't spill if I accidentally knock it over, and it also keeps the water clean and at a constant temperature. I set myself a goal of drinking the whole bottle, and find it works best if I do this before starting any of my other practices. It gives me the boost and the energy I need to meditate, journal and carry out other practices.'

– Kate

Chapter 7

Exercise

'Lack of activity destroys the good condition
of every human being, while movement
and exercise save it and preserve it.'

– Plato

We're pretty sure you already know that regular exercise is good for you. As humans, we are designed to move. But for many of us, our lives have become increasing sedentary – spending much of our working days stuck behind a desk, before slumping in front of a screen at night.

Building some physical activity into your morning routine helps to wake you up and gets things moving. This has important physical, emotional and mental benefits that last throughout your day.

These six S.H.I.N.E. practices offer a range of ways you can reconnect with your body and get it moving, creating energy, vitality and flexibility for the day ahead.

- Body scan (page 151)
- Dancing (page 156)
- Making your bed (page 159)
- Movement (page 163)
- Shaking (page 167)
- Yoga (page 171)

Choose any of these practices – think about what will best suit your body. If you want a suggestion for where to start, we propose making your bed and shaking as quick and easy places to begin.

Body scan

'Go inside and listen to your body,
because your body will never lie to you.'

– Don Miguel Ruiz, *The Four Agreements*

Your body is always talking to you. The question is, are you listening to it? And when you do listen, do you act on what you hear?

We tend to spend a lot of the time in our heads, disconnected from our bodies. This means that we miss a lot of important information about ourselves and our health and wellbeing.

Moving your awareness slowly through your body is a powerful technique to reconnect with yourself and your needs, making you more present and centred as you start a new day.

The goal of this practice is to explore and tune in to the physical sensations of your body.

The intention is not to change or fix anything, but simply to be present and listen to what your body has to say.

Sometimes noticing physical sensations and giving them consideration is all it takes to lessen their intensity and the effect they have on your daily life.

And as you become more experienced and comfortable with body scanning, you'll become more attuned to your body and its needs. If, for example, tight shoulders are a warning sign that you're becoming stressed, you'll notice this sooner and be able to take action to calm yourself before things become more serious.

There is increasing scientific evidence that body scanning has physical and mental health benefits. One 2019 study published in the *Mindfulness* journal found that people who did a mindful body scan every day for eight weeks had lower levels of the stress hormone cortisol, and also reported feeling less stressed.

In doing this, body scanning boosts your immune system, meaning the body is more resilient and less prone to disease.

How to shine with body scanning

- Find a comfortable sitting or standing position.

- Close your eyes and take a few deep, slow, gentle breaths. Allow your breathing to settle into a natural rhythm.

- Relax and turn the focus of your attention inwards. Carry on breathing slowly and gently.

- Let your awareness lightly scan through your body. Start from the soles of your feet and work slowly upwards, body part by body part, to the crown of your head, as follows:

- toes and feet
- ankles, lower legs and knees
- thighs, hips and pelvis
- stomach and chest
- back (lower, middle, upper) and shoulders
- upper arms, elbows and forearms
- wrists, hands and fingers
- neck and throat
- face (mouth, ears, nose, cheeks, eyes and forehead)
- whole head, right up to the crown

As you scan, tune in to your body to notice any sensations that arise.

What do you notice? Does anything feel cold or warm? Does anything feel heavy or light? Or tingling or tight? Does anything have a particular texture, colour or shape?

Don't try to change anything, just be curious and open to anything you feel.

Don't worry if you find it hard to notice

much at first. That's OK. You are training yourself to listen to your body, and this might take practice.

○ When sensations arise, softly rest your focus there. Breathe into them.

○ If the sensation could speak, what might it say to you?

○ Wait to see if an answer arises. Try not to anticipate or decide what this answer will be. Just wait.

○ The answers may surprise you. They may even seem silly or irrational. Do not judge them. We are dealing with instinct and intuition, not logic. Just accept what comes up and reflect on this. (You may choose to act upon it later, if you feel able to.)

○ If nothing comes up, accept that too. The answer may come later or not at all. That's also fine.

○ Start by taking about three minutes to complete your body scan. Set yourself a timer (if you are using your phone for this, remember to put it on 'do not disturb' mode). As you get more familiar with this practice, you might want to extend the time you spend on it.

Afterwards, you might find it useful to take a few minutes to reflect on or write down what you noticed. This can help you to identify patterns and changes over time.

'In the Western world, many people have become disconnected (almost "disembodied") from themselves. I see this a lot when working with business leaders. At first, some find the idea of a body scan rather alien. However, over time, most find it powerful – and sometimes moving – to reconnect with their whole self. They discover it helps them become more in control of their emotions, because they are more tuned in to their feelings, and therefore the early warning signs of stress and disease. As a result, they are able to make conscious choices to get themselves back in balance. This helps not only them, but also those around them.'

– Kate

Dancing

'We should consider every day lost in
which we have not danced at least once.'

– Friedrich Nietzsche, *Thus Spoke Zarathustra*

Most of us will unconsciously start to move when we
hear a beat, perhaps by tapping a foot, drumming a
finger or nodding our head in time to the music.

This is because our bodies are designed to dance. We
instinctively respond to music with movement. Think
about the unconscious way babies move when they hear
a happy tune, or how a familiar song can magically
awaken old memories or reanimate an elderly relative.

The more you enjoy the music, the stronger your urge
to move in time with it.

Dancing wakes you up, gets your energy flowing and
puts a smile on your face. And unlike many other forms
of movement, it offers a total body workout. Dancing not
only enhances your circulation, it also increases flexibility, and muscle strength and tone.

And dancing offers more than just physical and
emotional benefits – it's a smart move. Research under-
taken by Stanford University shows that dancing gives
your brain an incredible workout, improving your
thinking processes and boosting your intelligence.

This is because it uses lots of parts of the brain simultaneously.

So why not dance your way into your day?

How to shine with dancing

○ Let go of any limiting beliefs you might have about your ability (or perceived inability) to dance. This practice is about having fun, not about scoring a perfect ten on the dancefloor.

○ You can dance anywhere – around your bedroom, on your way to the shower, or even in the kitchen while you're waiting for the kettle to boil.

○ Just put on some fun and uplifting music and start moving along to it. Wiggle, jiggle, jump around – whatever you fancy.

○ Give yourself permission to be free in your dancing. Dance like a child. Be silly. Express yourself however you want to.

○ Dance as if nobody's watching. Dance for the sheer joy of dancing. Just dance!

☀ Sing along, too, if it makes you feel good.

☀ Dance on your own, or get others involved (in person or online) and make it a family affair.

☀ You might want to create a special playlist of morning music that will make you feel like dancing into your day. You could create different playlists for different days of the week or seasons of the year.

☀ If you are worried about the noise disturbing other people, try dancing with headphones on, silent-disco style.

'One of my best friends loves to dance as she makes breakfast for her kids. Often, the kids dance with her too, and they all laugh and giggle away for a few minutes at the start of their day. No one cares *how* they dance: it's the taking part that matters. When I go to stay there, it's one of the highlights of the day – the fun is infectious!'

– Kate

Making your bed

'If you make your bed every
morning, you will have accomplished
the first task of the day.'

– Navy SEAL Admiral William H. McRaven

Believe it or not, there are positive benefits to be had from the simple practice of bed-making. We like to see this as a form of exercise, because it's an easy way to get your body up and moving first thing in the morning. And this helps make it feel more beneficial and less like a chore.

The movements that come with this practice can encourage your body to awaken and start to release tension. It's an easy and gentle way to activate your energy.

What's more, evidence shows that making your bed increases your productivity. This is because you are taking charge of yourself and your day right at its very start, as you get out of bed. This gives you a small but significant sense of pride in yourself and your surroundings.

This micro-step, which only takes a minute or so, will encourage you to take on other small tasks. Adopting a keystone habit like making your bed kick-starts a chain of positive decisions and actions throughout your day.

By the evening, you may find that this easily completed task has turned into many other successes. We know this to be the case, because so many of our clients have told us of their surprise at the difference this simple practice has made.

If you work from home, in or near your bedroom, this practice is even more important, as external mess *around* you tends to create internal mess *within* you. So, if you want to bring a greater sense of calm and order to your mind, start by creating calm and order in your surroundings.

Plus, once your bed is made, you are much less likely to decide to crawl back into it! A made bed incentivises you to get up and get going. It forms a boundary marker between sleep and action for the day ahead.

What's more, at the end of the day, your bed is ready for you to climb into and enjoy a good night's sleep, renewing your energy for the next day. You can see it as a gift from your morning self to your evening self.

A poll by the National Sleep Foundation found that people who made their bed every day were almost 20 per cent more likely to get a good night's rest. And, given how important sleep is to how we feel in the morning, this is further impetus to do it.

How to shine by making your bed

- Making your bed doesn't have to mean doing it with military precision. Whether you prefer sheets and blankets or a duvet, it's simply about making it look neat, tidy and inviting.

- Use this as an opportunity to get active. Move around as you make your bed. Shake out your duvet. Plump up your pillows. Smooth down your covers. Maybe even change your sheets.

- We don't think you need much more guidance on *how* to do this. Just encouragement to actually do it. Think about the difference it could make to your whole day.

- So, give it a try and see – it'll only take a minute to do. And the rewards can be great.

'You may have spent your teenage years being told to tidy your room and make your bed – I certainly was! And nowadays, I find myself frequently telling my teenage son, Nathan, to make *his* bed (not always successfully). However, I now make my own bed every day, without fail, as soon as I get up. It's a small but key part of my morning routine. And, interestingly, reading the first draft of this book inspired our mum to start making her bed as soon as she gets up every day, which she had long ago stopped doing. From small things, great things grow, so who knows what other changes that may lead to for her.'

– Kate

Movement

'It is exercise alone that supports the spirits, and keeps the mind in vigour.'

– Marcus Tullius Cicero

We all know that movement and exercise are good for us. The evidence is undeniable. They offer improvements in strength, balance, flexibility and motor skills, and help us with maintaining a healthy body weight.

Now, you may have expected that. But you may not be aware of all the other ways in which moving your body is shown to help.

Regular exercise brings better quality of sleep, increased energy levels, effective pain management and improved quality of life. It has also been shown to promote positive mental health. Among other things, it is proven to help reduce anxiety and depression.

According to Sport England, the many gains to be had from physical exercise include reducing the risk of developing type 2 diabetes by 30–40 per cent, as well as significantly reducing the risk of developing many other medical conditions, including stroke, cancer and dementia.

What's more, it helps your brain function. When you exercise your body, it exercises your brain, and as your brain starts to work more, the pathways within it grow stronger. This improves the way you process information, and strengthens your memory. It also leads to a lowering of blood pressure and resting heart rate, which boosts your physical health, too.

And did you know there is evidence that exercising in the morning provides benefits that you cannot obtain from exercising at any other time of the day?

Morning movement helps release tension from the body, gets your circulation going and boosts your metabolism. It also improves your mood and raises your energy levels, enabling you to think better and concentrate for longer throughout the day ahead.

Recent research shows that as little as seven minutes of high-intensity exercise done in the comfort of your own home, with no special equipment, produces physical benefits similar to those of several hours of running or cycling.

How to shine with movement

> The important thing is to get your body moving at the start of the day. This can be when you first wake up, while you're still in bed, immediately after you get up, or a bit later, when you feel a little more awake. Experiment – see what works best for your morning routine.

The hardest thing with exercise is getting started. So, to encourage you to do this, try laying out your exercise clothes and shoes the night before, ready to put on as soon as you get up. A client was finding it hard to do the exercise he planned, and simply 'found himself' watching the television instead. Toby suggested he stick a big sign over the screen of his TV saying, 'Don't just turn me on. Go for that run!' to motivate him in the mornings. It worked.

There are lots of different ways you can exercise in ten minutes or less, if that's all you've got – and, of course, for longer, if you have the time. These include going for a brisk walk or run, doing a high-intensity interval workout, resistance training, cycling or spinning, dancing (see page 156), shaking (see page 167), yoga (see page 171), Pilates, or even just performing a few simple stretches, or walking up and down the stairs a few times. Anything that gets you going will help.

Be guided by what's right for you. Listen to your body. Make sure you warm up first before trying anything too strenuous.

☼   If you have any concerns at all, please consult
    your doctor or other medical professional
    before starting any new form of exercise.

'The way I exercise has had to change a lot over
the years as my life and body have changed. In my
twenties, I used to get up early and go horse-riding
before work. In my thirties, I started doing Pilates,
as well as running and attending gym classes. I've
had a lot of issues with my knees, hips and back
over the years. I've learned to listen to my body and
I am not able to go running nowadays, so I do a
combination of yoga, Pilates, stretching and brisk
walking, depending on how my body feels and
what my schedule allows. It is the balance between
these that is key for me – so I vary them across the
week. What matters is that I do something to get me
moving, even if it's just for a few minutes.'

– Kate

Shaking

> 'Stop a minute, right where you are.
> Relax your shoulders, shake . . . like a
> dog shaking off cold water. Tell that
> imperious voice in your head to be still.'
>
> – Barbara Kingsolver

Have you ever wondered why cats, dogs and many other animals enjoy a good shake when they wake up? It's because they instinctively know it helps to release tension, relieve stiffness from sleeping and get the body ready for action.

Most of us know how tight and 'locked' our bodies feel when we're worried, stressed or anxious. We all have our own unique patterns of holding muscular tension in the body – it might be a restriction in your neck and shoulders, a tightening in your stomach, or a clenching of your hands. In turn, this impacts our behaviour – resulting in irritability, loss of temper, poor decision-making and unhelpful habits, like excessive drinking.

There are a growing number of clinical studies into the benefits of shaking (or 'self-induced tremors') and initial findings suggest that it appears to work by rewiring our nervous systems. The act of deliberately shaking appears to hack the body's natural reflexes, quite literally helping us to loosen and let go of our default physical holding patterns of stress.

Shaking also stimulates the body's circulatory systems. However, this isn't about going for the burn or raising your heart rate. It's about gently getting your body moving, releasing any blockages, so that your energy can flow more freely.

How to shine with shaking

- Stand with your feet firmly on the floor, about hip width apart.

- Breathe naturally and keep your joints soft throughout.

- Allow your arms to hang loose and heavy by your sides. Allow your shoulders to lower and relax downwards.

- Start by gently shaking your right hand. Take the shaking up through your right wrist, forearm, elbow, upper arm and all the way to your shoulder. Keep shaking your arm for around fifteen seconds, then slow the shaking and bring your arm back to rest gently by your side.

Do the same with your left arm.

Next, take your weight on to your left foot and gently raise your right foot. If you feel wobbly, rest your hand on the back of a chair or against the wall. Start by shaking your right foot, then move the shaking slowly up through your calf, knee, thigh, buttock and up to your hip. Gently shake the whole of your leg for around fifteen seconds, then slow the shaking and bring your leg back down to the floor.

Repeat with your other leg.

Now gently shake the whole of your body – arms, legs, bum, hips and shoulders – in any way that feels good to you.

You may wish to finish by shaking your arms up above your head, and then gently folding forward from the hips as you continue gently shaking your torso and arms. Allow the whole body to relax and release as you hang there shaking.

Gently slow the shaking and ease yourself back upright.

☼ Many of our clients and students find it helpful to imagine any blocks, tightness or tension falling out and away from the body as they move – like shaking stones out of a shoe. Enjoy the wonderful sense of release and freedom this brings to your body and your mind.

☼ Remember to be gentle. If anything feels tight or uncomfortable, shake that part more slowly and gently, in a way that feels right for you. Stop at any time, if you feel the need to.

'I always start my Dru Yoga classes with some gentle shaking before moving on to the yoga sequences and postures. People are frequently surprised at just how effective shaking can be in releasing tightness and tension. It's also brilliant for literally shaking off frustrations and irritations. I love to imagine that I'm shaking away any cares or concerns before I step, feeling lighter and brighter, into the rest of my day.'

– Toby

Yoga

'Yoga is the journey of the self,
through the self, to the self.'

– the *Bhagavad Gita*

Yoga is an ideal way to gently wake up your body and mind at the start of the day. It has been practised for thousands of years to bring health, happiness and harmony. It originated in ancient India and became popular in the West during the twentieth century.

In the West, yoga is most often associated with the physical practice of postures (or *asanas* in Sanskrit) to build flexibility, and strengthen and relax the body. However, this is only one aspect of yoga.

A full yoga practice actually includes physical postures, sequences of movement, breathing techniques and meditation. It also encompasses your overall approach to life.

Yoga is about balance, not balancing on one finger or looking perfect. The word 'yoga' comes from Sanskrit and means 'to join'. Thus, yoga is the practice of bringing the mind, body and emotions into union.

There are many different styles of yoga, each with their own flavour, emphasis and approach. Everyone can find a style of yoga to practise, whatever their age, body type, or level of fitness and flexibility.

Dru Yoga makes an ideal morning practice. It's a graceful and therapeutic form of yoga that gently combines mindful movement, breath and relaxation. And it really works. People who regularly practise Dru Yoga report a range of remarkable benefits:

- 89 per cent are better able to handle stress
- 84 per cent regularly experience less body tension
- 91 per cent say that it transforms negative thinking
- 69 per cent report that they have more positive sleep patterns
- 72 per cent experience an improvement in their back pain
- 93 per cent enjoy greater flexibility in their spine and joints

In 2019, a comprehensive research review found that practising yoga increases activity in areas of the brain involved in learning, memory, dealing with stress and managing emotion. The evidence is clear. By practising any form of yoga, you're not only helping your body stay healthy, you are also actually developing your brain.

How to shine with yoga

If you're new to this practice, try out a range of approaches to choose the style of yoga that suits you best. The key is to find one that helps brings you back into balance.

It may be helpful to join a local class or online studio so that you are taught by a qualified yoga teacher. That way, you'll safely learn some simple movements that can become part of your morning routine.

If you already practise yoga, try doing a few sun salutations (*surya namaskara*) to welcome the day – but be sure to warm up your body before trying anything too strenuous. The aim is to *release* tension, not create it.

Here is a short and effective yoga sequence that Toby teaches his students and clients as a way to start the day.

You can do these movements either standing or sitting (in a chair or on the edge of your bed). Either way, the key is to keep the movement smooth and flowing, avoiding any sense of stress or strain on your joints and muscles.

Sit or stand with your feet a comfortable distance apart. Feel yourself firmly connected to the ground beneath you, with your weight evenly balanced across both your feet.

☀ Start by gently bringing the palms of your hands together in front of your chest, with the fingers pointing upwards.

☀ Become aware of your breath and allow it to settle into a natural rhythm as you move through the sequence.

☀ Breathing in, lift your hands up towards the ceiling, opening your arms out into a wide 'Y' shape and allowing your breastbone to gently lift.

☀ Pause briefly. Feel the expansion, and enjoy a sense of filling yourself with vitality for the day.

☀ Breathing out, slowly bring your palms together above your head, then lower them back down the centre of your body in front of your chest as you fold forward from the hips, coming down into a forward bend. Only go as low as feels right for you.

☀ Release your hands and allow them to relax down towards the ground, hanging loose.

○ Pause briefly. Feel the sense of acknowledging and letting go of yesterday to create space for today.

○ Bending your knees, raise yourself gently back up to standing as you allow your spine to unfurl. Bring the palms of your hands together in front of your chest again, back to where you started.

○ Repeat the sequence as many times as feels right to you each morning. We suggest you do at least three rounds of it. Keep moving at your own pace and intensity. Allow it to flow – don't force or push anything.

○ As you continue flowing with the movements, you may wish to try silently saying or thinking 'yes' on the in-breath and 'thank you' on the out-breath. You could also visualise opening yourself up to the energy of a new day as you breathe in and letting go of the cares of yesterday as you breathe out.

○ On the final out-breath, complete the sequence by gently bringing your palms together in front of your chest, with the fingers pointing upwards. Take a moment to notice the way you feel more centred and energised.

☼ If you have any concerns at all, please consult your doctor or other medical professional before starting any new form of exercise.

'Dru is a gently flowing and powerfully effective style of yoga. It's suitable for all ages, abilities, shapes and sizes. I love how it has helped me and so many others to transform their lives. My students range from schoolchildren to senior citizens. One of my oldest students is ninety-one, and she says yoga is why she is "still going" after all these years. Who am I to disagree?'

– Toby

Part 3

Rising and shining every morning

'Knowledge is of no value unless you put it into practice.'

– Anton Chekhov, *A Life in Letters*

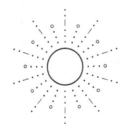

Chapter 8

Crafting your S.H.I.N.E routine

'Knowing is not enough; we must apply.
Willing is not enough; we must do.'

– Johann Wolfgang von Goethe

Congratulations on getting here. Now it's time to craft your personal S.H.I.N.E. routine. We suggest allowing anything from fifteen minutes to an hour for your new routine.

All good routines need a structure, and it's the same with S.H.I.N.E. While S.H.I.N.E. is not a prescriptive approach, you'll benefit most from building a routine that comprises a range of practices. It's all about finding an equilibrium to bring your wellbeing back into balance.

One way to do this is to pick one practice from each of the five S.H.I.N.E. sections. This will ensure you have a balanced and varied routine. As you use the practices, you'll find that a number of them complement each other and work particularly well together. There may be times, though, when you gain most benefit from focusing on one or two of the specific S.H.I.N.E. sections. You'll find more guidance on this in the next chapter.

> 'Imagine for a moment that you wanted to improve your fitness. If you did biceps curls every day, your arms would definitely get stronger. But your overall fitness would not improve as much as it would if you combined these biceps curls with running, sit-ups and stretching. And your health and fitness would improve even more if you also ate a healthy diet. It's the same with your morning routine. Any one practice will help, but the real power comes from combining them into a well-rounded routine.'
>
> – Kate & Toby

Your S.H.I.N.E planner

We know that you are 42 per cent more likely to achieve your goals if you write them down. Remember: 'Don't just think it, ink it!'

For this reason, we have provided a simple S.H.I.N.E. planner to help you craft and capture your routine.

It is most helpful to write the practices in the order in which you will do them. This provides a simple-to-follow schedule for your morning routine.

Keep a copy on your bedside table or hang it on the wall nearest your bed so you'll see it as soon as you wake up.

S.H.I.N.E. Practice	S	H	I	N	E	Preparation/ things needed	Time needed	Notes
List the S.H.I.N.E. practice you have chosen to work with, e.g. free writing.	X					Make a note of any preparation required or things you will need for the practice, e.g. a notebook and pen.	Write down the number of minutes you will spend doing the practice, e.g. 10 minutes	You might want to note down your plans for your practice, or keep a note of things you have found helpful, e.g. "I've found writing at a table or desk easier than resting on my lap.'

Sample S.H.I.N.E. starter routines

To help you get going, we have created a couple of sample routines using the practices we suggest as good starting points in each of the five S.H.I.N.E. sections.

We share a blank S.H.I.N.E. planner and examples of our personal S.H.I.N.E. planners in the Resources section.

Starter routine one

S.H.I.N.E. Practice	S	H	I	N	E	Preparation/ things needed	Time needed	Notes
Alarm clock (page 96)			X			Set alarm the night before.	1 minute	Count backwards from 5 when the alarm goes off, then get up!
Smiling (page 91)		X					1 minute	Fake it 'til you make it ☺.
Structured journaling (page 62)	X					Put the journal and pen on the bedside table the night before.	10 minutes	
Making your bed (page 159)					X		1 minute	
Breakfast (page 125)				X		Make sure there is food for breakfast.	10 minutes	Vary it from day to day.

Starter routine two

S.H.I.N.E. Practice	S	H	I	N	E	Preparation/ things needed	Time needed	Notes
Water (page 145)				X		Fill my water bottle and put it on the bedside table the night before.	1 minute	Drink immediately upon waking.
Breathing (page 37)	X						3 minutes	
Gratitude (page 73)		X					3 minutes	Remember to choose 5 new things each morning.
Mapping your day (page 111)			X				5–10 minutes	Write down schedule in calendar to refer back to during the day.
Shaking (page 167)					X		3 minutes	Nice to do this to music.

Polishing your S.H.I.N.E. routine

Like so many things in life, the more time and effort you invest in your morning S.H.I.N.E. routine, the greater the rewards you will reap.

Experiment and be willing to allow your routine to change and grow alongside you and your life. As you start to notice the benefits, try introducing additional practices, as time allows.

Most importantly, enjoy it and make your mornings something you look forward to. This way, when the alarm goes off on a cold winter's morning and the bed feels especially warm and inviting, you'll get up for your S.H.I.N.E. routine with eagerness and enthusiasm, because you know it holds the key to a great day.

Chapter 9

Rising and shining through life's changes and challenges

How to make S.H.I.N.E. work for you

'Keep the breath of the new dawn and
make it part of you. It will give you strength.'

– Hopi proverb

Humans feel more at ease when we have certainty. As the world we live in becomes increasingly unpredictable, we can feel more and more overwhelmed and out of control. This frequently leads to feelings of worry and anxiety, and negatively impacts our wellbeing and mental health.

This is why a morning routine is even more import-ant in times of change, challenge and uncertainty. It doesn't matter whether these are things we have chosen for ourselves – such as starting a new job, adapting to a different way of working, moving home or entering a new relationship – or if they are things that are happening *to* us – like a relationship break-up, illness or injury, bereavement, job loss or a major world event.

'Remember that both you and your needs will change as your life changes, and your morning S.H.I.N.E. routine can adapt to reflect this. We've found that what works best on a cold, dark morning doesn't always work so well on a bright summer's day; what's useful on a busy work day may not give you what you need at the weekend; and what helps when you have to start early for work will be less beneficial on days where you are free to create your own schedule.'

– Kate & Toby

Balancing your 'wellbeing see-saw'

Wellbeing is about more than just work–life balance. We find it helpful to think of it like a see-saw. It moves up and down based on the challenges and the resources we have at any particular time in our lives.

These challenges are the demands that drain our mental, physical and emotional energy, while our resources are the things that boost our health and well-being: the things that give us energy, vitality and zest for life, and help us rise and shine. We flourish when our wellbeing see-saw is in equilibrium.

When life and work are more challenging, we need to build and strengthen our resources to even things out. This is what your morning S.H.I.N.E. routine does for you. It ups your wellbeing resources to counteract the weight of the demands on you.

If you are struggling right now, using the S.H.I.N.E. practices can help you to get back on an even keel. If you feel like you are just surviving, it can help you start thriving. If you already feel good, you'll feel even better.

Shining through new ways of working

More and more of us find ourselves working in new and different ways. For many of us this involves working at home, all or some of the time. If we do have a workplace to go to, mobile technology means we are still connected, even when we are not physically there. While there are undoubtedly some benefits to this, it all too often means the boundaries between our work and our personal lives become blurred, leaving us feeling like we are always 'on'. When work bleeds into our personal lives, it raises our stress levels, damaging our wellbeing and mental health.

Effective management of the transitions between our work and personal lives is key to reducing our stress levels. A study by the University of Illinois found that having control over our boundaries softens the spikes in stress caused by the intrusion of work into our lives and homes.

Your S.H.I.N.E. routine enables you to shape a helpful transition between sleep and work. It's not about being rigid: it's about finding ways to create boundaries that work for you. Some of the practices are specifically designed to help you with creating and marking these boundaries, both in the morning and throughout your day.

When you are struggling to make the transition from sleeping to working, you may find it especially helpful to consider some of the following practices:

- Alarm clock (page 96)
- Free writing (page 47)
- Making your bed (page 159)
- Mapping your day (page 111)
- Shaking (page 167)
- Structured journaling (page 62)

You'll discover further suggestions of S.H.I.N.E. practices and routines to suit different circumstances and challenges later in this chapter.

Creating a virtual commute

Traditionally, the journey from our homes to our places of work has given us the dedicated time and space in our day to transition from home to work.

When you don't travel to work, you could choose to use some or all of this time for your new S.H.I.N.E. routine instead, to carve out time and space for yourself before you move into your working day. Think of this as a virtual commute.

This might mean getting out of the house and moving before coming back home to start work. The S.H.I.N.E. practices that are helpful here include movement (page 163), nature (page 137) and sunlight (page 141).

Many commuters use their journey to do things they enjoy, like reading, listening to music and podcasts, or watching a favourite programme. Another way to see the virtual commute is as a chance to bring these activities back into your morning, in particular through joy (page 78) and learning (page 129).

This is your opportunity to create your ideal 'journey' to work. Get on board and see where it takes you.

Shining when life gets tough

We all have times in our lives when things feel tough. Perhaps you are super busy and rushed off your feet? Maybe you're facing some difficult changes? Perhaps you're lacking focus and motivation? It could be you don't know where or how to start? You might have slept really badly and feel exhausted?

In the table below, you'll find suggestions to help you navigate the challenges we all face from time to time.

You can use all the practices in the order suggested to make up a full S.H.I.N.E. routine, or just pick one or two of them: whatever feels most supportive and helpful for you. Use the S.H.I.N.E. planner (page 182) to help you create your routine.

These are just suggestions to get you started. Take some time to experiment and find what works best for you: what most enables you to feel lighter, brighter and inspired for the day ahead. And remember to revisit and refresh your routine as your life, work and needs evolve.

Your challenges	S.H.I.N.E. practices to boost your resources
Do you have a long, busy day ahead of you?	1. Alarm clock (page 96) 2. Breathing (page 37) 3. Mapping your day (page 111) 4. 'To-be' list (page 119) 5. Breakfast (page 125)
Are you feeling overwhelmed by everything you need to do?	1. Meditation (page 52) 2. Mantra (page 133) 3. Goal-setting (page 106) 4. Mindset (page 115) 5. Creative visualisation (page 101)
Do you need structure and direction?	1. Making your bed (page 159) 2. Structured journaling (page 62) 3. Goal-setting (page 106) 4. Mapping your day (page 111) 5. Creative visualisation (page 101)
Are you lacking in motivation?	1. Making your bed (page 159) 2. Structured journaling (page 62) 3. Mindset (page 115) 4. Learning (page 129) 5. Movement (page 163)
Did you sleep badly and now feel tired and grumpy?	1. Water (page 145) 2. Body scan (page 151) 3. Smiling (page 91) 4. Sunlight (page 141) 5. Dancing (page 156)

Your challenges	S.H.I.N.E. practices to boost your resources
Are you finding it hard to wake up and get going in the morning?	1. Alarm clock (page 96) 2. Water (page 145) 3. Joy (page 78) 4. Shaking (page 167) 5. Nature (page 137)
Are you worried, stressed or anxious?	1. Gratitude (page 73) 2. Mindfulness (page 58) 3. Positive affirmations (page 86) 4. Shaking (page 167) 5. Mapping your day (page111)
Are you feeling sad and low?	1. Candle gazing (page 43) 2. Gratitude (page 73) 3. Smiling (page 91) 4. Mirror work (page 82) 5. Joy (page 78)
Do you feel lonely and disconnected?	1. Hugging (page 68) 2. Free writing (page 47) 3. Gratitude (page 73) 4. Yoga (page 171) 5. Nature (page 137)

Chapter 10

Making S.H.I.N.E. your habit

How to embed your new morning routine

'Renew yourself completely each
day; do it again, and again,
and again. Forever again.'

– traditional Chinese proverb

You can change.

It turns out the old saying, 'You can't teach an old dog new tricks,' is wrong.

We used to think that our brains stopped changing once we reached adulthood. We now know that they continue to grow and adapt throughout our lives. What's more, we have the power to shape these changes: to quite literally rewire our brains through the way we choose to think, feel and act.

Imagine walking into a field of long grass, with a clear path across the middle of it. As you walk into that field, the instinctive (and easiest) thing to do is to follow that well-worn path. But you don't *have* to do this. You can consciously choose to walk a different route. At first, you might have to trample your way through the undergrowth. You may encounter some bumps and holes along the way. But if you keep a clear sense of where you are going, you'll reach the other side of the field safely. And in so doing, you'll start to create a new path.

The next day, when you come to this field, you will still need to consciously take the new route, rather than the old well-worn path. But, over time, if you do this every day, the grass will begin to grow back over the old route, and the new path you are forming will become clearer and clearer. This is essentially what happens in your brain as you start to make different choices. New neural pathways become stronger and old ones weaken.

Take care not to sabotage yourself

Watch out for old patterns of resistance, self-sabotage or setting yourself up to fail. These may include some or all of the following. See if you recognise any of these well-worn paths in yourself and your own behaviour:

- an urge to just do what's easy, familiar or comfortable
- a tendency to procrastinate or put off starting your new routine 'until tomorrow'
- that voice in your head that says, 'What's the point? It won't work for me,' or 'It's too late for me to change now'
- the need to be perfect and not get things wrong
- the desire to do everything, all at once
- the expectation of seeing instant results, and a tendency to give up too soon if you don't
- a proclivity to get easily bored and lose enthusiasm
- an inclination to worry about what other people will think

Remember neuroplasticity – just because this is how things have been for you in the past, it doesn't mean they have to be the same in the future. You have the power to change, the power to choose a different way. You have the opportunity for a new beginning, starting right NOW.

The learning process

The things we are in the habit of doing feel familiar and comfortable to us, even if they are not actually helping us. Doing something new or different requires us to move out of this 'comfort zone'.

So when you begin a new practice, it takes a bit of effort and some time for it to feel natural. Don't let this put you off. You need to get used to it, rather like wearing new shoes that initially feel uncomfortable, but settle in after a few wears.

> 'I often use the example of learning to drive a car to help my clients understand the learning process. Before you learn to drive, you have high hopes. You're excited. You've seen people driving; it looks pretty easy. Or maybe you're nervous, not sure of what to expect. The technical name for this is 'unconscious incompetence' – you don't realise what you don't know.
>
> Then you have your first driving lesson. It's over-whelming, maybe even scary. It all feels incredibly complicated. There are so many things to do at the same time. You feel stupid. Will you ever be able to master this? This is the stage of 'conscious

incompetence' – where you become painfully aware of how much there is to learn. Some people give up at this stage.

But if you want to master driving, you need to keep going. To keep practising, allowing yourself to make mistakes so you gradually improve. Through doing this, you reach the stage of 'conscious competence' – you can do it, but it takes a lot of focus and energy. (Hopefully you are at this stage when you take your driving test!) And then, through the ongoing application of the things you have learned (i.e. by driving regularly) it becomes more and more natural. You have reached the stage of 'unconscious competence'. Much of the driving process is now instinctive. Driving starts to flow. You can look around and enjoy the journey as you drive.'

– Kate

How we form new habits

Learning to rise and shine is all about cultivating new positive morning habits.

We know that repetition is important when it comes

to forming new habits, as it creates the new pathways in our brains. This is because repetition strengthens the connections between our brain cells, so that they communicate better with each other.

We also know that emotion is key to this. When your brain associates a positive feeling with an action, it takes notice of this, and it will help you remember to do it again. And you'll be more likely to want to repeat it, so that you can feel those positive emotions once more.

It's a virtuous cycle. The more happy, engaged and joyful you feel when you do your morning practices, the better you'll be at rewiring your brain to maintain this new habit in your life.

When you need a bit of support

From time to time, we all need a bit of support and encouragement.

For some of you, your S.H.I.N.E. routine will feel personal and private, but others might find it helpful to share what you are doing with a partner or close friend. You could ask them to check in with you regularly to help you stay motivated. One of our good friends schedules a morning call with someone who acts as an accountability partner for her when she needs a bit of extra motivation.

Another option is to buddy up with someone to share your experiences of using the S.H.I.N.E. method. That way, you can keep each other company, stay on track and learn from one another's experience.

Ten simple steps to S.H.I.N.E.

Based on the latest findings from neuroscience, combined with our many years of experience supporting people to change, here are our 'Ten simple steps to S.H.I.N.E.'.

1. Remember your 'why'

Your end goal is not the routine itself: it's the difference it makes to your day. We form new habits more quickly when we're clear about our motivation to change. Remember why you created your S.H.I.N.E. routine: the benefits it brings to you and your life.

What's your motivation for doing this? Do you want to improve your sense of wellbeing? Be more productive? Shine through and rise above life's challenges and changes? Become the best version of yourself each and every day? Remind yourself of this whenever you need to.

2. Create time and space

Carve out some time for your routine at the start of your day – maybe set your alarm just a little bit earlier.

Try to find a space where you can focus without distractions for these few precious minutes. Reduce competition for your attention in your environment. Put your phone on 'do not disturb' and shut out all sources of digital distraction.

We strongly suggest that you do your S. H. I. N. E. practices before you start looking at messages, social media and emails.

3. Set yourself up to succeed

Make it easy to do your routine. The fewer barriers you have to getting started, the easier it is to do.

It can also be helpful to set a daily diary reminder. Think of this as making an appointment with yourself.

The night before, you might like to prepare anything you will need for your morning practices, such as putting your journal and pen on your bedside table, laying out your workout clothes, or prepping a healthy breakfast. This creates less work for your brain, as you won't have to make choices when you wake up – you can just get going straight away. It also means you'll be less likely to find reasons not to complete your chosen practices.

4. Be realistic

Set standards that are achievable for where you are right now. Work out how much time you can realistically dedicate to your morning S.H.I.N.E. routine (we recommend anything upwards of fifteen minutes). Pick a combination of practices you can actually do in this time. Don't set yourself up to fail by trying to do to more than is feasible. It's better to start small and build from there.

5. Be consistent

Consistency helps.

Your environment and your behaviour are linked. When you walk into the bathroom in the morning, you know you are there to use the loo, shower or brush your teeth. The brain makes the association between the context and the activity. This is known as an 'action trigger'. Use this principle to help your S.H.I.N.E. routine stick by practising your routine at the same time and in the same place each morning.

6. Have fun

You are more likely to stick with your routine if you enjoy doing it. Pick practices that make you feel good. Enjoy the process. Be playful. This is not about doing things perfectly, it is about 'practising'. Give yourself permission to try things out, make mistakes and learn. Have fun with it!

7. Take it one day at a time

You only ever need to focus on one day at a time. Each day, make a commitment to start that morning with your S.H.I.N.E. routine.

On days when you feel busy and overwhelmed, don't give up. These are the days when you most need to take care of yourself and set yourself up to succeed. This is not about self-indulgence; it's about doing what supports you to be at your best. Remember your 'wellbeing see-saw'. When life gets tough, you need to do the things that give you the energy and resilience to help keep you in balance.

Even if you can only spare a few minutes, just pick one practice. Give yourself the gift of one small thing to help you shine through the difficult day ahead.

8. Celebrate small wins

Be positive and encouraging to yourself. Acknowledge and celebrate the positive differences you are bringing into your life, one morning at a time.

Give yourself a mental pat on the back each day for

the changes you are making. Research shows that the positive feelings you evoke by doing this rewire your brain, making you want to do more of whatever it is that has given you these positive feelings. This will not only help you to feel good, it will also motivate you to embed and benefit fully from your new routine.

9. Stick with it

Give the practices a chance to feel natural and work for you. If you want to shine, you have to keep taking action, again and again. That's why the techniques we have shared with you are called *practices*: they don't work in *theory*, they work when you *practise* them and use them regularly.

Keep going. Complete your routine, even on the days when you don't feel like doing it. It's the repetition that counts. The good news is, the more you keep practising, the easier it gets.

If you miss a day or two, don't let that set you back. It doesn't matter – unless you make a habit out of it. Just start again the following morning. After all, tomorrow is another day.

10. Review and refresh

After a few weeks, review how your S.H.I.N.E. routine is working for you.

What differences are you finding in your levels of calmness, happiness, wellbeing, focus, energy and productivity? What other changes are you noticing? Which practices are you particularly enjoying using?

Continue with your current S.H.I.N.E. routine for as long as feels right for you. As your life changes, you are likely to want to adapt things. You might try adding or replacing practices to refresh it and keep it fun and interesting – and to keep you rising and shining.

Shine brightly

Thank you so much for reading *Rise and Shine*. We have really enjoyed sharing the S.H.I.N.E. method with you.

These practices have transformed our lives and those of many others we have worked with over the years.

By using S.H.I.N.E. to change your mornings, you truly can change your life.

Rise higher and shine brighter, day by day.

Resources

Tools to help you S.H.I.N.E.

'Shine like the whole universe is yours.'

– Rumi

This section contains tools and planners to help you create and polish your new morning S.H.I.N.E. routine.

We also share with you our own S.H.I.N.E. routines – both long and short versions – with some notes on why and how these practices work for us.

- The 30 S.H.I.N.E. practices (page 208)
- Your S.H.I.N.E routine planner (page 209)
- Our own S.H.I.N.E routines (pages 212–221)

The 30 S.H.I.N.E. practices at a glance

S	H	I	N	E
Silence	Happiness	Intention	Nourishment	Exercise
To bring stillness, peace and reflection into your morning	*To help you move into your day with a smile on your face*	*To create your day, rather than letting your day create you*	*To feed your mind, body and soul*	*To create energy and flexibility for the day ahead*
Breathing	Hugging	Alarm clock	Breakfast	Body scan
Candle gazing	Gratitude	Creative visualisation	Learning	Dancing
Free writing	Joy	Goal-setting	Mantra	Making your bed
Meditation	Mirror work	Mapping your day	Nature	Movement
Mindfulness	Positive affirmations	Mindset	Sunlight	Shaking
Structured journalling	Smiling	'To-be' list	Water	Yoga

Your S.H.I.N.E. routine planner

You'll find it helpful to write the practices that make up your new S.H.I.N.E. routine in the order in which you will do them. This way, you create a simple-to-follow schedule for your mornings. You will find a blank planner and some examples of our S.H.I.N.E. routines on the following pages.

S.H.I.N.E. Practice	S	H	I	N	E	Preparation/ things needed	Time needed	Notes
List the S.H.I.N.E. practice you have chosen to work with, e.g. free writing.	X					*Make a note of any preparation required or things you will need for the practice, e.g. a notebook and pen.*	*Write down the number of minutes you will spend doing the practice, e.g. 10 minutes*	*You might want to note down your plans for your practice, or keep a note of things you have found helpful, e.g. 'I've found writing at a table or desk easier than resting on my lap.'*

S.H.I.N.E. Practice	S	H	I	N	E	Preparation/ things needed	Time needed	Notes

Example 1: Kate's current S.H.I.N.E. routine

S.H.I.N.E. Practice	S	H	I	N	E	Preparation/ things needed	Time needed	Notes
Alarm clock (page 96)			X			Set alarm the night before.	1 minute	I like to change it around, sometimes using a favourite song, wind chimes or birdsong as my alarm.
Water (page 145)				X		Take water to bed the night before	1 minute	I have a small bottle of water beside my bed so I can reach for it as soon as I wake up.
Sunlight (page 141)				X			1 minute	I like to open the blinds as soon as I wake up to start the day with natural light (if the time of year allows).
Breathing (page 37)	X						5 minutes	My breathing practice calms and rebalances me like nothing else. I particularly like to work with alternate nostril breathing.

S.H.I.N.E. Practice	S	H	I	N	E	Preparation/ things needed	Time needed	Notes
Positive affirmations (page 86)		X				Affirmation list	3 minutes	*I read my current list of affirmations – sometimes aloud and sometimes in my head.*
Structured journaling (page 62)	X					Notebook and pen	10 minutes	*I sit silently, without distractions, and journal, reflecting on a number of questions. This always includes what I am grateful for and some form of goal or intention-setting for the day ahead. (See gratitude, page 73, and goal-setting, page 106.)*
Making your bed (page 159)					X		1 minute	*I always make my bed; this creates a sense of calm and order, and signals that it's time to move into more active practices.*

Example 1: Kate's current S.H.I.N.E. routine

S.H.I.N.E. Practice	S	H	I	N	E	Preparation/ things needed	Time needed	Notes
Movement (page 163)					X		10–15 minutes	*I get myself moving. It is particularly important for me to keep myself healthy and rebalance my body after a night in bed. Depending on how my body is feeling, sometimes this is gentle, and at other times more vigorous.*
Breakfast (page 125)				X		Food for breakfast	5–10 minutes	*I always have something fresh and nourishing to eat – even if it's just a piece of fruit.*

Example 2: Kate's 'short-for-time' S.H.I.N.E. routine

S.H.I.N.E. Practice	S	H	I	N	E	Preparation/ things needed	Time needed	Notes
Alarm clock (page 96)			X			Set alarm the night before.	1 minute	I like to change it around, sometimes using a favourite song, wind chimes or birdsong as my alarm.
Water (page 145)				X		Take water to bed the night before	1 minute	I have a small bottle of water beside my bed so I can reach for it as soon as I wake up.
Positive affirmations (page 86)		X				Affirmation list	3 minutes	I read my current list of affirmations – sometimes aloud and sometimes in my head.
'To-be' list (page 119)			X				2 minutes	I go through the day ahead and reflect on how I need to be to get the most out of it.

Example 2: Kate's 'short-for-time' S.H.I.N.E. routine

S.H.I.N.E. Practice	S	H	I	N	E	Preparation/ things needed	Time needed	Notes
Making your bed (page 159)					X		1 minute	I always make my bed; this creates a sense of calm and order, and signals that it's time to move into more active practices.
Breakfast (page 125)				X		Food for breakfast	5–10 minutes	I always have something fresh and nourishing to eat – even if it's just a piece of fruit.

Example 3: Toby's current S.H.I.N.E. routine

S.H.I.N.E. Practice	S	H	I	N	E	Preparation/ things needed	Time needed	Notes
Water (page 145)				X		Take water to bed the night before	1 minute	*I'm not a fan of icy cold water at the best of times, but especially not during the colder months. So I take an insulated bottle of water up to bed with me. That way, I have warm water at hand, ready to start my first practice.*
Candle gazing (page 43)	X					Candle and matches	5 minutes	*I light my (World Peace Flame) candle as soon as I get out of bed. I like the feeling of having started my day with an intention of peace and light. I keep it burning while I am doing my other practices.*

Example 3: Toby's current S.H.I.N.E. routine

S.H.I.N.E. Practice	S	H	I	N	E	Preparation/ things needed	Time needed	Notes
Nature (page 137)				X			1 minute	*Most days, I need to get up to let our sausage dog, Lennie, out. I use this as an opportunity to breathe in some fresh morning air and gaze up at the sky.*
Meditation (page 52)	X						15 minutes	*I will meditate, if only for a few minutes, each morning.*
Creative visualisation (page 101)			X				5 minutes	*This may be visualising myself successfully navigating the day ahead or achieving special goals (e.g. writing Rise and Shine).*
Joy (page 78)		X				A book	5–15 minutes	*Reading is my go-to joy practice. As a child, I was late in learning to read, so I'm making up for lost time now. It makes me happy.*

S.H.I.N.E. Practice	S	H	I	N	E	Preparation/ things needed	Time needed	Notes
Making your bed (page 159)					X		1 minute	When I make my bed in the morning, it's like a gift to myself for when I come home later that evening.
Yoga (page 171)					X	Yoga mat	10–15 minutes	I listen to my body and adapt my practice to suit its needs. Sometimes these are just simple stretches, while on other days I'll complete more dynamic sequences and postures. I like to listen to mantras while doing yoga.
Breakfast (page 125)				X		Food for breakfast	10–15 minutes	I never skip breakfast. This is as much for others as for me, as when I'm hungry, I get tired and irritable.

Example 4: Toby's 'short-for-time' S.H.I.N.E. routine

S.H.I.N.E. Practice	S	H	I	N	E	Preparation/ things needed	Time needed	Notes
Alarm clock (page 96)			X			Set alarm the night before.	1 minute	*I rarely set an alarm, unless I'm getting up especially early. If I do set one, I'll find an alarm tone that wakes me gently or makes me smile.*
Water (page 145)				X		Take water to bed the night before	1 minute	*I take an insulated bottle up to bed with me. That way, I have hot water at hand, ready to start my first practice.*
Candle gazing (page 43)	X					Candle and matches	1 minute	*I light my (World Peace Flame) candle as soon as I get out of bed. When time is short, it's only lit for a few minutes while I'm doing my other practices and getting ready for the day ahead.*

S.H.I.N.E. Practice	S	H	I	N	E	Preparation/things needed	Time needed	Notes
Gratitude (page 73)		X					5 minutes	If I'm busy, my meditation becomes a gratitude practice, reflecting on all the people, places and things in my life for which I'm thankful.
Making your bed (page 159)					X		1 minute	When I make my bed in the morning, it's like a gift to myself for when I come home later that evening.
Breakfast (page 125)				X		Food for breakfast	10–15 minutes	I never skip breakfast. When I'm hungry, I get tired and irritable.

Notes and references

Here you will find sources for the quotes and the research evidence we have referenced throughout the book, along with further reading recommendations.

INTRODUCTION

Angelou, M. [@DrMayaAngelou]. (17 May 2013). https://twitter.com/DrMayaAngelou

Cain, A. (24 November 2017). '6 morning routines that are hard to adopt but will pay off for life'. *Independent*.

Ritschelin, C. (5 September 2018). 'The 27-minute morning routine that could change your life, according to science'. *Independent*.

PART 1 - STARTING TO SHINE

Warhol, A. (1975). *The Philosophy of Andy Warhol: From A to B and Back Again*. Harvest/HBJ.

CHAPTER 1: OUR STORIES

Priestley, J.B. (1956). *All About Ourselves: And Other Essays*. Heineman.

CHAPTER 2: THIS IS YOUR WAKE-UP CALL

Vivekananda, S. (1947). *Complete Works of Swami Vivekananda*. Advaita Ashram.

Elrod, H. (2016). *The Miracle Morning*. John Murray Learning.

Rothbard, N. P. (21 July 2016). 'How your morning mood affects your whole workday.' *Harvard Business Review*.

Spall, B. & Xander, M. (2018). *My Morning Routine*. Penguin.

PART 2: THE 30 S.H.I.N.E. PRACTICES

Oliver, M. (1992). *New and Selected Poems, Vol. One*. Beacon Press.

CHAPTER 3: SILENCE

Introduction

Beaumont, A. (21 April 2017). '10 reasons why silence really is golden'. *Psychology Today*.

Gregoire, C. (9 January 2017). 'Why silence is so good for your brain'. www.huffpost.com

Gross, D. (7 July 2016). 'This Is Your Brain on Silence'. www.nautil.us

Breathing

André, C. (15 January 2019). 'Proper breathing brings better health'. *Scientific American*.

DiSalva, D. (29 November 2007). 'How breathing calms your brain, and other science-based benefits of controlled breathing'. *Forbes*.

Doll, A. (1 July 2016). 'Mindful attention to breath regulates emotions via increased amygdala-prefrontal cortex connectivity'. *NeuroImage*, 134, 305–313.

Harvard Health Publishing. (13 April 2018). 'Relaxation techniques: Breath control helps quell errant stress response'. www.health.harvard.edu

Muktibodhananda, S. (1985). *Hatha Yoga Pradipika*. Yoga Publications Trust.

Candle gazing

Frank, A. (1952). *The Diary of a Young Girl*. Vallentine Mitchell.

MacCuish, S., Patel, M. & Wells, A. (2003), *The Flame That Transforms*. Life Foundation Publications.

Mindvalley. (17 January 2019). 'The Hypnotic Lure of Candle Meditation: A Gentle Way to Stillness'. www.blog.mindvalley.com

Patel, M. (2000). *The Secret Power of Light*. Life Foundation Publications.

Raghavendra B. R. & Ramamurthy V. (2014). 'Changes in heart rate variability following yogic visual concentration (*Trataka*)'. *Heart India, 2*,15–18.

Rajpoot, P., & Vaishnav, P. (2014). 'Effect of *Trataka* on anxiety among adolescents'. *World Academy of Science, Engineering and Technology, International Journal of Psychological and Behavioral Sciences, 8*(12), 4004–4007.

Free writing

Ackerman, C. (12 December 2020). '83 benefits of journaling for depression, anxiety and stress'. www.positivepsychology.com

Baikie K. A., Wilhelm K. (2005) 'Emotional and physical health benefits of expressive writing'. *Advances in Psychiatric Treatment, 11*(5), 338–346.

Cameron, J. (1994). *The Artist's Way: A Course in Discovering and Recovering your Creative Self*. Souvenir Press.

Cameron, J. (2017). *The Right to Write: An Invitation and Initiation into the Writing Life*. Hay House UK.

Smyth, J. M., Stone, A. A., Hurewitz, A. & Kaell, A. (1999). 'Effects of writing about stressful experiences on symptom reduction in patients with asthma or rheumatoid arthritis: a randomized trial'. JAMA, 281(14), 1304–9.

Meditation

Dass, R. (1971). *Be Here Now*. Crown Publications.

Easwaran, E. (2010). *Words to Live By*. Nilgiri Press.

Gaudin, M. (2014). *The Meditation Experience*. Bounty Books.

Goleman, D. & Davidson, R.J. (2017). *The Science of Meditation*. Penguin Life.

Khalsa, D.S. & Stauth, C. (2001), *Meditation as Medicine*. Astria.

Sevinc, G., Hölzel, B. K., Greenberg, J., Gard, T., Brunsch, V., Hashmi, J. A., Vangel, M., Orr S. P., Milad, M. R. & Lazar, S. W. (2019). 'Strengthened Hippocampal Circuits Underlie Enhanced Retrieval of Extinguished Fear Memories Following Mindfulness Training'. *Biological Psychiatry* 86(9), 693–702.

Mindfulness

Hanh, T. N. (1975). *The Miracle of Mindfulness*. Rider.

Hanson, R. & Mendius, R. (2009). *Buddha's Brain: The Practical Neuroscience of Happiness, Love & Wisdom*. New Harbinger.

Kabat-Zinn, J. (2013). *Full Catastrophe Living*. Piatkus.

Kabat-Zinn, J. (2005). *Wherever You Go, There You Are*. Hyperion.

Khalsa, D.S. & Stauth, C. (2001). *Meditation as Medicine*. Astria.

Shapiro, S., Oman, D., Thoresen, C., Plante, T., & Flinders, T. (2008). 'Cultivating Mindfulness: Effects on Well-Being'. *Journal of Clinical Psychology, 64*(7).

Wax, R. (2016). *A Mindfulness Guide for the FRAZZLED.* Penguin Life.

Williams, M. & Penman, D. (2011). *Mindfulness: A Practical Guide to Finding Peace in a Frantic World.* Piatkus.

Structured journaling

Fritson, K. (2008). 'Impact of journaling on students' self-efficacy and locus of control'. *InSight: A Journal of Scholarly Teaching, 3.*

Jose, P., Lim, B. & Bryant, F. (24 April 2012). 'Does savoring increase happiness? A daily diary study'. *Journal of Positive Psychology, 7*(3).

Power, M. (21 July 2017). 'Dear Diary ... The surprising health benefits of journaling'. *Telegraph.*

Purcell, M. (8 October 2018). 'The health benefits of journaling'. www.psychcentral.com

Smyth, J. M., Johnson, J. A., Auer, B. J., Lehman, E., Talamo, G. & Sciamanna, C. N. (2018). 'Online positive affect journaling in the improvement of mental distress and well-being in general medical patients with elevated anxiety symptoms: a preliminary randomized controlled trial'. *JMIR Mental Health, 5*(4).

Sontag, S. (2009). *Reborn: Journals and Notebooks.* Picador.

Watson, R., Fraser, M. & Ballas, P. (Date unknown). 'Journaling for Mental Health'. www.urmc.rochester.edu

CHAPTER 4: HAPPINESS

Introduction

Achor, S. (2010). *The Happiness Advantage: The Seven Principles that Fuel Success and Performance at Work*. Virgin Books.

Holden, R. (1998). *Happiness Now!*. Hodder and Stoughton.

Lama, D. & Cutler, H. C. (2009). *The Art of Happiness: A Handbook for Living*. Hodder & Stoughton.

Sare, R. (1701). *Marcus Aurelius (Emperor of Rome)*.

Seppälä, E. (2017). *The Happiness Track: How to Apply the Science of Happiness to Accelerate Your Success*. HarperOne.

Hugging

Buscaglia, L. (2017). *Living, Loving and Learning*. Prelude.

Cirino, E. (10 April 2018). 'What are the benefits of hugging?'. www.healthline.com

Ducharme, J. (3 October 2018). 'Science says you should embrace hugging'. *Time*.

ENELL. (24 May 2019). 'Embrace the 20-second hug for better health'. www.enell.com

Killam, K. (17 March 2015). 'A hug a day keeps the doctor away'. *Scientific American*.

Satir, V. (1988). *The New Peoplemaking*. Science and Behaviour Books.

Gratitude

Beattie, M. (3 December 2017). 'Gratitude turns what we have into enough'. www.melodybeattie.com

Beattie, M. (1990). *The Language of Letting Go*. Hazelden FIRM.

Emmons, R. A. & McCullough, M.E. (2003). 'Counting blessings versus burdens: An experimental investigation of gratitude and subjective wellbeing in daily life'. *Journal of Personality and Social Psychology, 84.*

Fredrickson, B. (2009). *Positivity.* Crown.

Mills, P.J. et al., Wood, A. & Chopra, D. (2015). 'The role of gratitude in spiritual well-being in asymptomatic heart failure patients'. *Spirituality in Clinical Practice, 2*(1), 5–17.

Morin, A. (3 November 2014). '7 scientifically proven benefits of gratitude that will motivate you to give thanks year-round'. *Forbes.*

Seligman, M. (2017). *Authentic Happiness.* Nicholas Brealey Publishing.

Walia, A. (14 February 2019). 'Scientists show how gratitude literally alters the human heart & molecular structure of the brain'. www.collective-evolution.com

Wong, J. & Brown, J. (6 June 2017). 'How gratitude changes you and your brain'. *Greater Good Magazine.*

Joy

Campbell, J. & Moyes, B. (1989). *The Power of Myth.* Bantam Doubleday Dell.

Coyle, D. (27 August 2017). 'How being happy makes you healthier'. www.healthline.com

Seppälä, E. (15 July 2013). 'The science behind the joy of sharing joy'. *Psychology Today.*

Thaik, C. (27 March 2014). 'A joyful life supports good health'. www.huffpost.com

Lama, D. & Tutu, D. with Abrams, D. (2016). *The Book of Joy.* Hutchinson.

www.laughteryoga.org

www.telephonelaughter.co.uk

Mirror work

Baker, N. (25 June 2012). 'Smile, you're on Yoko Ono's new app'. www.reuters.com

Hay, L. L. (2011). *Mirror Work: 21 Days to Heal Your Life*. Hay House.

Raypole, C. (27 September 2020). 'The beginner's guide to mirror gazing meditation'. www.healthline.com

Well, T. (5 August 2018). 'Why Is Seeing Your Own Reflection So Important?'. www.psychologytoday.com

Positive affirmations

Crane, P. (2002). *Ordering from the Cosmic Kitchen*. The Crane's Nest.

Hay, L. (2010). *Experience Your Good Now!: Learning to use Affirmations*. Hay House.

Hay, L. (1984). *You Can Heal Your Life*. Hay House.

Moore, C. (12 October 2020). 'Positive daily affirmations: is there science behind it?'. www.positivepsychology.com

Yuko, E. (14 May 2019). 'The surprising effects of mantras on our focus and productivity'. www.thriveglobal.com

Smiling

Hanh, T. N. (2011). *Your True Home*. Shambhala Publications.

Selig, M. (25 May 2016). 'The 9 superpowers of your smile'. *Psychology Today*.

Spector, N. (28 November 2018). 'Smiling can trick your brain into happiness — and boost your health'. www.nbcnews.com

Chapter 5: Intention

Introduction

Murphy, Paul, A. (29 October 2013). 'The science of smart: how the power of intention can help you learn better'. www.pbs.org

Salzberg, S. (1 August 2014). 'The power of intention'. *O Magazine.*

Weindling, M. (13 June 2017). 'The science of intention'. www.upliftconnect.com

Alarm clock

Harvey-Jenner, C. (2 April 2019). 'Why snoozing your alarm could be damaging your health'. *Cosmopolitan.*

Hoff, V. (12 October 2018) 'This is what happens to your body when you keep hitting snooze'. www.thethirty.com

Jones, K. (2019). *222 Ways to Trick Yourself to Sleep.* Piatkus.

Creative visualisation

Brenner, A. (25 June 2016). 'The benefits of creative visualization'. *Psychology Today.*

Clarey, C. (22 February 14). 'Olympians use imagery as mental training'. *New York Times.*

Gawain, S. (1978). *Creative Visualization.* New World Library.

Walker, Stephen. (2007). 'Using mental imagery to improve the return from sport injury'. www.podiumsportsjournal.com

Goal-setting

Boss, J. (19 January 2017). '5 reasons why goal setting will improve your focus'. *Forbes.*

Gardner, S. & Albee, D. (2015). 'Study focuses on strategies for achieving goals, resolutions'. Press Releases. 266. www.scholar.dominican.edu/news-releases/266

Locke, E.A. (2002). 'Setting goals for life and happiness'. *Oxford Handbook of Positive Psychology*. Ed. S.J. Lopez & C.R. Snyder. Oxford University Press.

Van Edwards, V. (6 December 2017). 'The science of goal setting'. www.huffpost.com

Mapping your day

Anzaldua, G. E. (2012). *Borderlands/La Frontera*. Aunt Lute Books.

American Psychological Association. (2 March 2006) 'Multitasking: Switching costs'. www.apa.org

Bregman, P. (20 February 2009). 'An 18-minute plan for managing your day'. *Harvard Business Review*.

Mindset

Baluku, M.B., Kikooma, J.F. & Otoo, K. (26 January 2017). 'Positive mindset and entrepreneurial outcomes'. *Journal of Small Business and Entrepreneurship, 30*(6).

Brown, B. (2013). *Daring Greatly: How the Courage to Be Vulnerable Transforms the Way, We Live, Love, Parent and Lead*. Portfolio Penguin.

Brown, B. (2010). *The Gifts of Imperfection: Let Go of Who You Think You're Supposed to Be and Embrace Who You Are*. Hazelden.

Dweck, C. (2012). *Mindset: How You Can Fulfil Your Potential*. Robinson.

Ng, B. (26 January 2018). 'The neuroscience of growth mindset and intrinsic motivation'. *Brain Sciences, 8*(2).

Peale, N. V. (1990). *The Power of Positive Thinking*. Cedar Books.

'To-be' list

Bradshaw, J. (2006). *Healing the Shame that Binds You*. Heath Communications.

Rice, C. (7 November 2017). 'Forget your to-do list – create a 'to-be' list'. www.huffpost.com

Salmansohn, K. (2 December 2010). 'Do be do be do? make your to-be list before your to-do list'. www.oprah.com

CHAPTER 6: NOURISHMENT

Introduction

Angelou, M. (1989). *Conversations with Maya Angelou*. University of Mississippi.

Neff, K. (2011). *Self-Compassion*. Yellow Kite.

Breakfast

Ducharme, J. (30 January 2019). 'Is breakfast really good for you? Here's what the science says'. *Time*.

Gardner, M., Wansink, B., Kim, J. & Park, S. (2014). 'Better moods for better eating? How mood influences food choice'. *Journal of Consumer Psychology, 24*.

Nazario, B. (27 December 2018). 'Breakfast: is it the most important meal?'. www.webmd.com

Ottolenghi, Y. (2018). *Simple*. Ebury Press.

Raichie, M. E. & Gusnard, D. A. (29 July 2002). 'Appraising the brain's energy budget'. *Proceedings of the National Academy of Sciences of the United States of America, 99*(16), 10237–10239.

Smith, A. P., Clark, R. & Gallagher, J. (1 August 1999). 'Breakfast cereal and caffeinated coffee: effects on working memory, attention, mood, and cardiovascular function'. *Physiology & Behaviour, 67*(1), 9–17.

Learning

Feinstein, L. & Hammond, C. (2004). 'The contribution of learning to health and social capital'. *Oxford Review of Education, 30.*

Feinstein, L., Vorhaus, J., & Sabates, R. (2008). *Mental Capital and Wellbeing: Making the most of ourselves in the 21st Century, in Learning through life: Future challenges.* Government Office for Science.

Hammond, C. (2004). 'Impacts of lifelong learning upon emotional resilience, psychological and mental health: fieldwork evidence'. *Oxford Review of Education.*

Psychologies. (22 June 2015). 'Want to be happier? Learn something new'. www.psychologies.co.uk

Mantra

Ashley-Farrand, T. (2000). *Healing Mantras.* Gateway.

Berkovich-Ohana, A., Wilf, M., Kahana, R., Arieli, A. & Malach, R. (2005). 'Repetitive speech elicits widespread deactivation in the human cortex: the "Mantra" effect?'. *Brain and Behaviour.* 5(7).

Nolan, J. (No date given). 'The science of mantras'. www. buddhaweekly.com

Swami, O. (2017) *The Ancient Science of Mantras.* Jaico.

Wei, M. (14 August 2015). 'How mantras calm your mind'. *Psychology Today.* www.krishnadas.com

Nature

Carrington, D. (13 June 2019). 'Two-hour "dose" of nature significantly boosts health – study'. *Guardian.*

Coles, J. (20 April 2016). 'How nature is good for our health and happiness'. www.bbc.co.uk.

Curie, M. (1923). *Autobiographical Notes: Pierre Curie with Marie Curie*. Dover Publications.

University of East Anglia. (6 July 2018). 'It's official – spending time outside is good for you'. www.neurosciencenews.com

Sunlight

Mead, M. N. (1 April 2008). 'Benefits of sunlight: a bright spot for human health'. *Environmental Health Perspectives, 116*(4).

Nall, R. (25 May 2018). 'What are the benefits of sunlight?'. www.healthline.com

Patel, M. (2000). *The Secret Power of Light*. Life Foundation Publications.

University of Edinburgh. (7 May 2013). 'Sunshine could benefit health and prolong life, study suggests'. www.sciencedaily.com

www.nhs.uk/conditions/seasonal-affective-disorder-sad/treatment/

Water

Adan, A. (2012). 'Cognitive performance and dehydration'. *Journal of the American College of Nutrition, 31*(2), 71–8.

NHS. (13 July 2011). 'Six to eight glasses of water "still best"'. www.nhs.uk.

Silver, N. (19 March 2019). 'Why is water important? 16 reasons to drink up'. www.healthline.com

CHAPTER 7: EXERCISE

Introduction

Dussault Runtagh, P. (14 March 2017). '6 evidence-based reasons why you should listen to your body'. www.huffpost.com

NHS. (11 June 2018). 'The benefits of exercise'. www.nhs.uk.

Body scan

Levey, J. & M. (2013). *The Fine Arts of Relaxation, Concentration, and Meditation.* Wisdom.

Ruiz, M. (1997). *The Four Agreements.* Amber Allen Publishing.

Schultchen, D., Messner, M., Karabatsiakis, A., et al. (2019). 'Effects of an 8-week body scan intervention on individually perceived psychological stress and related steroid hormones in hair'. *Mindfulness, 10,* 2532–2543.

Dancing

Nietzsche, F. (author) & Hollingdale, R. J. (trans.) (1974). *Thus Spoke Zarathustra.* Penguin Classics.

Heid, M. (4 July 2017). 'Why dancing is the best thing you can do for your body'. *Time.*

NHS Confederation. (22 September 2019). 'How dance improves physical and mental health'. www.nhsconfed.org

Making your bed

Duhigg, C. (2013). *The Power of Habit.* Random House.

The University of Texas at Austin. (16 May 2014). 'Adm. McRaven Urges Graduates to Find Courage to Change the World'. www.news.utexas.edu

Movement

Biddle, J. & Ekkekakis, P. (2005) 'Physically active lifestyles and wellbeing'. *The Science of Well-being.* Ed. Huppert, F., Baylis, N. & Keveme, B. Oxford University Press.

Reynolds, G. (9 May 2013). 'The scientific 7-minute workout'. *New York Times.*

www.sportengland.org

Shaking

Baylis, N. (6 November 2014). 'Mental wealth: rid yourself of the physical effects of negative emotions'. www.prweek.com

News in Health (1 January 2019). 'Shake it off – boosting your mood'. www.newsinhealth.nih.gov

Wimberger, L. (2015). *Neurosculpting: A Whole-Brain Approach to Heal Trauma, Rewrite Limiting Beliefs, and Find Wholeness.* Sounds True Inc.

Woodhall, V. (21 October 2018). 'Shaking is the stress-busting trend that everyone can benefit from'. www.getthegloss.com

www.kingsolver.com

Yoga

Barrington, C., Goswami, A. & Jones, J. (2010). *Dru Yoga: Stillness in Motion.* Dru Publications.

Dru Yoga. (2019). 'The benefits of Dru Yoga & meditation – Dru Yoga research results'. www.druyoga.com

Gothe, N.P., Khan, I., Hayes, J., Erlenbach, E. & Damoiseaux, J.S. (2019). 'Yoga effects on brain health: a systematic review of the current literature'. *Brain Plasticity,* 5(1), 105–122.

Patel, M., Barrington, C., MacCuish, S. & Jones, J. (1998). *The Dru Bhagavad Gita.* Life Foundation Publications.

Patel, M., Goswami, R., Barrington, C., MacCuish, S. & Rowan, L. (2014) *The Dance Between Joy and Pain: A Practical Guide to Emotional Wellbeing and Fulfilment.* Dru Publications.

Muktibodhananda, S. (1985) *Hatha Yoga Pradipika.*

PART 3: Rising and shining every morning

Chekhov, A. (author), Phillips, A. & Bartlett, R. (trans.) (2004) *A Life in Letters*. Penguin Classics.

CHAPTER 9: RISING AND SHINING THROUGH LIFE'S CHANGES AND CHALLENGES

Bulger, C.A., Matthews, R.A., & Hoffman, M.E. (2007). 'Work and personal life boundary management: Boundary strength, work/personal life balance, and the segmentation–integration continuum' *Journal of Occupational Health Psychology, 12*(4), 365–375.

Dodge, R., Daly, A., Huyton, J., & Sanders, L. (2012). 'The challenge of defining wellbeing'. *International Journal of Wellbeing, 2*(3), 222–235.

Ohu, E. A., Spitzmueller, C., Zhang, J., Thomas, C. L., Osezua, A., & Yu, J. (2019). 'When work–family conflict hits home: Parental work–family conflict and child health'. *Journal of Occupational Health Psychology, 24*(5), 590–601.

Park, L., Liu, Y., & Headrick, L. (2020) 'When work is wanted after hours: Testing weekly stress of information communication technology demands using boundary theory'. *Journal of Organisational Behaviour, 41*(6).

CHAPTER 10. MAKING S.H.I.N.E. YOUR HABIT

Fogg, B. (2019). *Tiny Habits: The Small Changes that Change Everything*. Virgin Books.

Goethe, J. W. (2014). *Faust: A Tragedy*. Yale University Press.

Milne, S., Orbell, S. & Sheeran, P. (2002). 'Combining motivational and volitional interventions to promote

exercise participation: Protection motivation theory
and implementation intentions'. *British Journal of Health
Psychology*, 7(2), 163–84.

Nastasi, A. (Date unknown). 'How long does it really take to
break a habit?'. www.hopesandfears.com

Phillippa, L., Jaarsveld, C., Potts, H., & Wardle, J. (16 July
2009). 'How are habits formed: Modelling habit formation
in the real world.' *European Journal of Social Psychology*, 40(6).

Acknowledgements

We would both like to thank the following for their encouragement, support, advice and love in helping us to write this book: our brilliant agent Clare Grist Taylor, our equally brilliant editor Bernadette Marron and the wonderful team at Little, Brown, our parents Peter and Yvonne Oliver, Matthew Bugg, Anna Wardley, Charlotte Murphy, Trisha Cochrane, Anthea Okereke, Kathryn McCullagh, Gill Farrer-Halls, and especially Jane Matthews whose HYL® workshop, assisted by Sharon Shingler, brought us together and sowed the seed that grew into this book.

Kate also wishes to specifically thank:

Dr Robert Holden, whose keynote speech at the Association for Business Psychology Conference 'woke me up' and first set me on my journey of personal transformation. Pete Cohen, whose coaching programme inspired me to change my mornings and thus my life. Liz Harrison, who shone her light on so many, myself included, and introduced me to the wonderful work of Louise Hay. The many other wise 'teachers' who have supported my personal and professional development over the years in becoming the person I am today, and those I am yet to meet. The numerous dear colleagues and friends whom I've had the joy to work with and learn from over the years (far too many to list and many of whom qualify in both categories). And special thanks, of course, to my son Nathan, my fiancé Nick and his daughter Lola, who light up my life every morning.

Toby also wishes to specifically thank:

Wendy Faulknall, my first yoga teacher, for introducing me to Dru Yoga and inspiring me to become a teacher myself. Dr Mansukh Patel and all my other wonderful Dru Yoga and Dru Meditation teachers and friends around the world. Dr Patricia Crane for her expert training and for bringing me into the worldwide Heal Your Life® family. Lotte Mikkelsen and Melanie Bloch for teaching me the joy of 'laughing for no reason'. Darren Brady and Ade Adeniji, whose 'The Quest for Gay Men' quite literally changed my life (for the better) in so many ways. I am also deeply grateful to Carole Wan and Alan Cooper, ACMH; Paul Denniston for the great gift of Grief Yoga™; and Dr Janey Fitzgerald for her wisdom, friend-ship and the joys of meditation. And an extra special thank you to my beautiful husband, Matthew, whom I still love waking up to after more than twenty-seven years together.

Above all, we offer heartfelt thanks to the many clients and students we've had the privilege to work with over the years. Thank you – you have taught us as much, if not more, than we have taught you.

Finally, we want to thank each other – writing this book has been a joy and a challenge. We have learned from each other and grown greatly through the process. The love, teamwork and commitment to each other has kept us going. We couldn't have done it alone, nor would we have wanted to.

About the authors

Kate and Toby Oliver are sister and brother.

Kate Oliver – BA (Oxon), C.Psychol. CPBP, AFBPsS

Kate has been working as a chartered psychologist and executive coach for nearly thirty years. She runs her own consulting business, KO Consulting Ltd (www. koconsulting.co), and has worked with thousands of leaders and their teams, in many prominent UK and global organisations.

Kate is passionate about helping others flourish in their lives and work. She uses her years of experience and psychological insight, combined with the latest advancements in neuroscience, to help her clients develop their capacity to learn and grow through challenges and change and enhance their wellbeing.

Kate is also a volunteer interview coach and stylist with Smart Works, supporting unemployed women in getting back into work. In her spare time, she loves to spend time in nature, practise Pilates and yoga and sing.

She lives in London and Hove with her son, Nathan, her partner, Nick, his daughter, Lola, and their English Toy Terrier, Pixie.

Toby Oliver – MA, RYT-500, MNCH & MNCP (Reg.)

Toby is an experienced teacher of yoga and meditation, qualified in Dru Yoga, Grief Yoga™, Laughter Yoga™ and Traditional Yoga (www.tobyyoga.com). He is also a registered therapist and Heal Your Life® Workshop trainer (www.eastviewtherapy.com). He works with groups in hospitals, hospices, charities and corporate organisations, as well as supporting individual clients. He specialises in helping adults and young people deal better with anxiety and serious or life-limiting illness, and to cope with grief and loss.

Toby began his career in cultural communications before co-founding Mr Bugg Presents, producers of the hit musical *Miss Nightingale*, which enjoyed five UK tours and a sell-out season in the West End. He has also co-written four professionally produced Christmas pantomimes.

Toby is proud to be a Stonewall School Role Model and gives regular talks in schools and colleges across the UK. He lives in Sheffield with his husband, Matthew and their wire-haired dachshund, Lennie.